For Christ's Sake Alone

Sake Alone

A Reformed, confessional, and devotional walk through the biblical doctrine of justification

J. D. Edwards

For your name's sake, O LORD,
pardon my guilt, for it is great.
(Psalm 25:11)[1]

---

[1] In this book, scripture is quoted in the English Standard Version, unless otherwise noted.

Endorsements

"Jason Edwards introduces us impressively to the key message of the Gospel: justification as God's great act of grace. With clear style, key Scripture passages, rich confessional quotes, in short, this book shows us again—or maybe even for the first time—what is central for the church, for theology and for each individual." —Dr. Herman Selderhuis, pastor, Luther, Calvin, and Puritan scholar, and professor at Theological University Apeldoorn, Netherlands

"In this wonderful little book, For Christ's Sake Alone, Jason Edwards opens up the truth of the doctrine of justification by faith alone. Carefully expounding texts of scripture, drawing forth important doctrinal principles, and applying the truths presented, Dr. Edwards presents the doctrine in simple and plain terms. Added to each chapter are helpful devotional thoughts to aid the reader. This is a great introduction to a fundamental tenet of our faith." —Dr. James M. Renihan, President, International Reformed Baptist Seminary

"Simple, doctrinal, devotional—these are the three words that come to mind as I reflect on Jason Edwards' helpful little book on the doctrine of justification. Whether you are a young Christian or a longtime believer just needing a firmer grasp of this key doctrine of the gospel, you would be helped by this short work." —Dr. Sam Waldron, pastor, author, professor, and President of Covenant Baptist Theological Seminary

For Christ's Sake Alone

"Pastor Jason Edwards has done Christ's church a good service in producing an accurate, astute, and accessible book on the important doctrine of justification. This book will be a useful reminder to those who already know and love this doctrine and a helpful guide to those who need to know." —Nick Clevely, pastor of Covenant Grace Baptist Church, New Zealand, and Co-host of Two-Age Sojourner Podcast

"Jason Edwards exhilarates the soul with colorful meditations on the nuts and bolts of justification. He depicts Christ as the lone drawbridge we hunted fugitives must cross over into a land of safety, Christ as a tide-drowned man on whom his younger brother stands until rescued, and Christ as the reliable place-reserver for starving orphans at the heavenly banquet table. Read it. You'll savor the Savior." —Mark Chanski, pastor, author, and Coordinator of Reformed Baptist Network

"Pastor Jason has taken the diamond of the doctrine of justification and examined it in the light of Scripture so that the reader has before their eyes the wonder of what it means to be saved by Christ alone." —Dr. Justin Miller, pastor of FBC Puxico and Director of Expositor Institute

Table of Contents

To the Reader

If you picked up this book, you likely fall into one of three categories.

(1) In the first group are you who want to know for certain that you are saved. You realize the stakes are too high to ignore this vital question: "Am I justified in the eyes of my Maker?" We will all face Him one day very soon after this short life. I pray that God will give you a new heart to believe. May you "know for certain that God has made him both Lord and Christ, this Jesus whom you crucified." (Acts 2:36) If you already enjoy salvation in Christ, then may God bless you with assurance as God elevates your view of Christ by your study here.

(2) You fall in the second category if you believe you are saved, but you want God to reform your understanding of this important truth by the authority of His word. The next step in your growth is to be cared for within a Confessional Reformed church. It is worth moving to another state or city to enjoy this. May you "not be conformed to this world, but be transformed by the renewal of your mind." (Romans 12:2) I pray for God to give you a sharp discernment about His truth.

(3) Finally, you may fall into a third category as one who will teach the doctrine of justification to others. I hope you will, and as you do, may this simple analysis be a resource to you in your labors. Remember, Paul sought to proclaim Christ and Him crucified — and suffered much for doing so — because justification is a battleground for the church in every generation. I pray "that you may be able to withstand in the evil day, and having done all, to stand firm." (Ephesians 6:13) This is your allotted time in which to stand for the truth of Christ, for His glory alone.

Doctrine means teaching. Our Lord Jesus calls Christians to become trained in good doctrine. "If you put these things before the brothers, you will be a good servant of Christ Jesus, being trained in the words of the faith and of the good doctrine that you have followed." (1 Timothy 4:6) Each chapter of this book focuses on one doctrine connected to the doctrine of justification. These doctrines are paraphrased from Chapter 11 of the Second London Baptist Confession of Faith of 1689, *Of Justification*, which you can read in full at the end of this book. An overview of each doctrine by chapter is provided next, to help you easily be able to reference whichever aspect of justification is most of interest to you at any point.

Overview Of Doctrines by Chapter

1. Mankind stands condemned on covenantal principles of federal headship and imputation.

2. God requires that you be justified before you can enjoy His glory.

3. Those whom God effectually calls He also freely justifies.

4. God is satisfied to pardon His people by Christ's death in their place.

5. God justifies sinners by imputing Christ's active obedience unto the whole law.

6. The Father is glorified in the Son's justifying work.

7. Live according to the truth that God counts Christ's righteous merits as your own.

8. The sole instrument of justification is faith. Faith is receiving and resting on Christ.

9. True saving faith is never found alone in the person justified — it is always accompanied by other saving graces worked by Christ's love within the believer.

10. God justifies for Christ's sake alone, not for anything in man.

11. You are justified in one distinct and irreversible moment: when the Holy Spirit applies Christ to you personally.

12. If justified, always justified. God continues to forgive the sins of those who are justified.

13. God has always justified His people in the same way, even before Christ's incarnation

and work. That is, by grace alone through faith in Christ alone.

To all who will read this, I pray that the riches of Christ, revealed in His word and upheld by our theological heritage, will glimmer before your heart's eye. Good theology leads to profound doxology. When Christ opened the eyes of the man born blind to see His Savior, the man's response was: "'Lord, I believe,' and he worshiped Him." (John 9:38) For this reason, each chapter on this glorious doctrine ends with a song and a prayer to guide you in responding to Christ your Savior. May your soul be nourished by Christ as a banquet feast as you commune with God in perfect peace, having been justified. If nothing else, dear Christian reader, when you ponder the question, "Why am I justified?" may the first thought that comes to your mind and comforts your heart be the phrase from our confession:

"I am justified for Christ's sake alone!"

For the glory of our King and the coming of His kingdom,

J.D. Edwards
Preaching Pastor
Reformed Heritage Church
Parker, Colorado

Chapter 1: The Story of Your First King

The Truth Shall Set You Free

Which would you rather:
a) to live in an imagined reality? Or
b) to know the ugly truth long ago about your family?

On one hand, an atheist philosopher named Thomas Nagel was surprisingly candid about his genuine preference. He wrote: "It is not just that I don't believe in God and hope that I am right in my belief. I hope there is no god. I don't want there to be a God. I don't want the universe to be like that."[2] On the other hand, a journalist adopted at an early age reflected as an adult about what she would like for her birth parents to know. Her reflection was along these lines: "Birth parents hold the key to an important part of who we are; we benefit when we are told the truth, no matter how ugly it may be."

You are reading this book because you want to know the truth. God has revealed the truth about our first parents. He has made it known to us in the Bible. To truly understand the significance of justification, you and I must first understand the story of our first king. Yes, the Bible teaches that you and I were born into an ancient story under the headship of a king.

You may be wondering, "When will this guy get to his point? What does Adam's story have to do

---

[2] Nagel, Thomas, *The Last Word*, pp. 130–131, Oxford University Press, 1997. Dr Nagel (1937–) is Professor of Philosophy and Law at New York University.

with my justification?" The Bible says in 1 Corinthians 15:22, "In Adam all die." We will appreciate the glorious doctrine of justification only if we understand how we all became cursed as heirs of Adam. So, we must first grab ahold of the principles by which we became condemned. Only then can we appreciate the principles by which we are justified.

You Are from The Line of This World's First King

At creation, God said, "Let us make man in our image, after our likeness. Let them have dominion over the fish of the sea, over the birds of the heavens, over the livestock, over all the earth, over every creeping thing on the earth." (Genesis 1:26) God made the world and pronounced it very good. Then, God gave Adam dominion over the world. Adam was the first king of this world. Adam's rule as king included dominion over the Serpent that creeps on the earth. He named it and reigned over it. Adam was the king, and the world was his kingdom. Here, God introduces believers to an important principle: *As goes the king, so goes his kingdom.*

God Appointed Your First King as A Prophet-Priest

Not only did God make Adam King, but He was also a prophet and a priest. Prophets spoke to the people on God's behalf. Prophets received direct revelation from God. In these ways, Adam was a prophet. But how was Adam a priest? To be a priest, Adam would need a temple in which to minister. Was this the case?

Genesis 2:8 says, "the LORD God planted a garden eastward in Eden; and there He put the man whom He had formed." (KJV) So Eden was a special place God created. Four rivers flowed from it, one in each direction. We can deduce that Eden was on a mountaintop, just as the temple would later be built on Mount Zion in Jerusalem. God also would later order the tabernacle and the temple to be decorated with trees and ornamental vegetation. Yahweh's temple on earth had the look of a garden. This look would have replicated God's design in Eden. "Out of the ground made the LORD God to grow every tree that is pleasant to the sight, and good for food; the tree of life also amid the garden, and the tree of knowledge of good and evil." (Genesis 2:9) So, Eden was a sort of mountain-top garden-temple with two special trees at its center. But how was Adam the priest?

We read in Genesis 2:15 that "the LORD God took the man, put him into the garden of Eden to work it (minister) and to keep it (guard)," Adam was especially placed by God inside this divine kingdom of heaven on earth. The two verbs that describe Adam's tasks in this temple garden are the same as those used to describe the work of Levites in Numbers 8:26. The priests were to "minister to their brothers in the tent of meeting by keeping guard." So, Adam's task was cultivation—the guarding, keeping, and expanding of the holy land of Eden, in which God's presence dwells until God's Sacred Garden temple fills the whole world with God's dwelling presence.

The Creator God Covenanted with Your First King

The Bible speaks of a "covenant" three hundred sixteen times across thirty-eight books. What is a covenant? A covenant is a perfect blend of law and love. One pastor described God's divine covenants as "more intimate and loving than a mere contract, more binding and accountable than a mere relationship." [3] Both Biblical and secular history record covenants between people.

One example of a covenant between men is Genesis 31:44-45. In this case, Laban said to Jacob: "'Come now, let us make a covenant, you and I. Let it be a witness between you and me.' Jacob took a stone and set it up as a pillar." Covenant commitments are remembered by a visual point of reference (like a pillar of stones). The visual representation of the covenant reminds every one of the commitments promised under oath. While this man-to-man covenant does not elaborate on the details, covenants contain these elements:

    a.   at least two parties.
    b.   promises or commitments made.
    c.   an oath with legal sanctions.
    d.   a visual representation.

If two or more of these elements exist, we ought to at least suspect a covenant. So, we can use this definition: *a covenant is an oath-bound promise, a legally sanctioned commitment.* The oath is a sanctioned because it legally binds rewards for obedience and curses for disobedience. A promise is

---

[3] Keller, Timothy. *Preaching: Communicating faith in an age of skepticism.* Penguin, 2016, p. 104.

just a promise. A law is just a law. What formalizes a covenant is sanctions.

The Bible says that Adam broke his covenant with God. The Lord says in Hosea 6:7: "Like Adam, they transgressed the covenant; there they dealt faithlessly with me." So, Adam was in a covenant with God. Do we see the elements of a covenant in the first few chapters of the Bible?

In Genesis 2:16–17, we read that "the Lord God…" So, God The Creator is one party as covenant Lord. And He "commanded the man…" So, man as a creature is the other party, the vassal servant. Next God establishes the terms of the covenant: "You may surely eat of every tree of the garden, but of the tree of the knowledge of good and evil you shall not eat." God's prohibition was an additional or "positive" law, above and beyond what was already naturally written on Adam's heart. Finally, the legal sanctions follow: "for in the day that you eat of it you shall surely die." Death was the covenant curse threatened for disobedience.

What was the promise offered as a reward for obedience? We read in Genesis 3:22-24 that God put angels and a flaming sword to guard access back into Eden, "lest he eat from the tree of life and live forever." From this, we can infer that eating from the Tree of Life was an additional blessing offered to Adam, which he could never again obtain. This is confirmed by Romans 3:23, which says that "all have sinned and fall short of the glory of God." We understand from these verses that God offered Adam further glory, beyond what he knew at creation.

However, Adam and all mankind fell short of the glory of God.

So, both trees together visually represent this first covenant of God with Adam. *The Tree of Life* represents the blessing that rewards obedience. *The Tree of the Knowledge of Good and Evil* represents the curse for disobedience. The Tree of Life offered Adam and all his posterity eternal life upon condition of his obedience. Had Adam obeyed, he would have constituted the many (all those who would come from him in natural generation) righteous. The Tree of the Knowledge of Good and Evil threatened death to Adam and all of his line for disobedience.

The Covenant of Works

All God's covenants with man are for His glory and our good. Adam already owed his Creator obedience. But the Creator God owed Adam nothing. God promised everlasting life to Adam in a special covenant. Because God created your first king sinless, his covenant was not gracious. God's covenant with Adam was kind, generous, and benevolent. God lovingly condescended to express Himself to Adam by way of covenant. Yet, by definition, grace implies de-merit. Adam did not need grace at creation because He had not de-merited any favor. For this reason, the church over the centuries has come to call this *The Covenant of Works*. Instead, if he worked for it by obeying God, he could merit for himself a further glory, a greater blessing.

One of the main editors of the 1689 Confession of Faith, Nehemiah Coxe,[4] explained it along these lines: God's covenant with Adam was the grounds for friendship between God and man. It promised rich bounty and goodness as a reward for obedience. But this covenant did not contain even an iota of pardoning mercy. If obeyed, it would raise man and his posterity to the high degree of the immortal angels in heaven. But if Adam disobeyed, his sin would sink all mankind to the low estate of apostate devils and leave him in a misery like theirs. Adam's obedience or disobedience became the trip wire. Adam's Covenant of Works governed entrance into a consummated cosmos.

Your First King Was A Federal Head

Because our first King, Adam, disobeyed by breaking God's covenant with him, all of Adam's natural posterity is born condemned under the curses of The Covenant of Works. The reverse is also true: if Adam had fulfilled His covenant of works, he would have secured all the blessings for himself and all those he represented. Romans 5:17 says: "Because of one man's trespass, death reigned through that one man." Adam was a federal head over all of his natural offspring.

God covenanted terms by which Adam was to bring all of creation into a state of secured blessedness. By Adam's obedience, the spiritual kingdom of perfect communion with God would cover all of the earth as much as it fills the heavens. Michael Reeves also saw the significance of this truth. He pointed out: If we deny Adam's place as a federal

---

[4] (paraphrased)

head of a covenant that would bring either blessing or condemnation upon all those he represents, then we lose the ability of all mankind to fall in Adam. If that is the case, we remove the reason for God's wrath against all of mankind's sins and trespasses. To deny Adam as a federal covenant head, is to undermine Christ's incarnation, Christ's imputation, and Christ's New Covenant.[5]

All mankind was represented in Adam. The key principle for justification is "imputation." This means that God puts the value or debt of one person on another. The only way to enter this world free of the imputed curse of the fallen federal head, our first king, would be if a man could somehow be conceived without the help of a sinful Son of Adam. This is because all men are under Adam's curse. All men, that is, with one exception: a man born of a virgin. As Collins put it: "A public head, so Adam stood, as Christ is of His spouse. And what he did as our chief head, we did it, whether by it we gain or lose."[6]

God's covenants are always for His glory and our good. This tragic story of our first king establishes God's principles of federal headship, imputation, and covenant sanctions. The chapters of this book aim to show how these principles make justification such good news for believers, for the glory of Christ alone.

[5] paraphrased from: *Should Christians Embrace Evolution?* ed. Norman Nevin and published by IVP -UK, 2009.
[6] Hercules Collins, *The Marrow of Gospel-History*. London: Printed by the Author (1696).

Chapter 2: The Great Hinge of Heaven's Gate

The Gospel Under Fire

Justification is the main feature of the gospel. It is the adoption certificate every child of God treasures. At the time of the Reformation, John Calvin put into words what all true Christians eventually realize: "Justification by faith is the hinge on which all true religion turns." [7] True religion is just as much under fire now as it was during the Reformation. The battleground is the "gospel of the glory of the blessed God with which [the true church] has been entrusted." (1 Timothy 1:11)

You might be thinking that if all Christians read the Bible, we ought to have uncontested unity on this vital point. Indeed, if you are a true believer, you will read the word of God with the help of the Holy Spirit within you, and His gospel truth will resound a faith-filled "Amen!" within your soul. "In the way of your testimonies I delight as much as in all riches." (Psalm 119:14) Yet, because justification is pivotal for true faith, for this very reason, it is attacked by Satan and those under his chains of darkness in every generation. The defense of scripture's precise teaching on justification has drained rivers of faithful martyr blood.

Jesus warned: "Beware of false prophets, who come to you in sheep's clothing but inwardly are

---

[7] John Calvin, *Institutes*, 3.11. p. 1.

ravenous wolves." (Matthew 7:15) To combat attacks from the enemy and false teachers throughout the history of the true church, Christ-loving shepherds have labored to express what the Bible does teach. We enjoy the spoils of previous wars in our creeds, confessions, and catechisms. Paul similarly warned the church: "Fierce wolves will come in among you, not sparing the flock." (Acts 20:29) Only with a firm grip on what the Bible really teaches about justification can you be fully equipped for the battle against sin, Satan, worldliness, and wolves. Let us receive God's word, then take up arms from our inherited arsenal to defend this pivotal truth.

Scripture Text: **Romans 3:23-26**

21 But now the righteousness of God has been manifested apart from the law, although the Law and the Prophets bear witness to it – 22 the righteousness of God through faith in Jesus Christ for all who believe. For there is no distinction: 23 for all have sinned and fall short of the glory of God, 24 and are justified by His grace as a gift, through the redemption that is in Christ Jesus, 25 whom God put forward as a propitiation by His blood, to be received by faith. This was to show God's righteousness, because in His divine forbearance He had passed over former sins. 26 It was to show His righteousness at the present time, so that He might be just and the justifier of the one who has faith in Jesus.

Context

In Romans 3, the apostle Paul makes clear to the Christians at the church in Rome (and to all who will read these God-breathed words) that Jesus Christ fulfilled all righteousness on behalf of His people. All of the Old Testament points to the righteousness of God unveiled in the person of Jesus Christ. Sinful mankind falls short of the glory of the just God. Yet, the just God became The Justifier! By grace alone, through faith in Christ alone, the righteousness of God is given to all who believe. "The great gospel blessing which Christ secures to such as believe in him is Justification."[8]

Doctrine

God requires that you be justified before you can enjoy His glory.[9]

The gospel is a simple message like a plain wooden door frame around a hole cut into a rocky mountain. "The law of the LORD is perfect, reviving the soul; the testimony of the LORD is sure, making wise the simple." (Psalm 19:7) After you enter the simple door frame of justification, you can enjoy the glory of God Himself! Justification opens up worlds of treasure, beauty, and mystery for the saved sinner — an eternity's worth.

Let us enter the simple door frame through a scriptural and time-tested definition. If you have not already, then please pause for a moment right where

---

[8] The New Hampshire Confession of Faith (1833), *V.*, Of Justification.
[9] Second London Baptist Confession of Faith (1677/89), *Chapter 11: Of Justification*.

you are. Prepare your heart to "enter His gates with thanksgiving, and His courts with praise! Give thanks to him; bless His name!" (Psalm 100:4)

Definition

"What is justification? Justification is an act of God's free grace, wherein He pardons all our sins, and accepts us as righteous in His sight, only for the righteousness of Christ imputed to us and received by faith alone."[10] Justification is bestowed solely through faith in the Redeemer's blood. Justification is the good news of "Him who loves us and has freed us from our sins by His blood." (Revelation 1:5) God does not bestow justification upon consideration of any works of righteousness done by a sinner. By our own works, we simply fall short of His glory. (Romans 3:23) Justification includes two blessings in Christ. First, the pardon of sin. In Christ, "you were washed, you were sanctified, you were justified in the name of the Lord Jesus Christ and by the Spirit of our God." (1 Corinthians 6:11) Second, the promise of eternal life on principles of righteousness. "God gave us eternal life, and this life is in His Son" (1 John 5:11)

The Doctrine Opened

Picture a man in the shadows, a fugitive in hiding. His eyes dart back and forth to survey his options for survival. He desperately wants to flee the misery of his war-torn nation. He watches from a distance the

---

[10] Benjamin Keach's Catechism (1666), Q. 37. See also Rom. 3:24; Eph. 1:7; 2 Cor. 5:21; Rom. 5:19; Phil. 3:9; Gal. 2:16.

border-crossing that separates the totalitarian regime where he was born and raised from the peaceful foreign nation on the other side of a deep, raging river. The only access point between the two countries is a drawbridge at the border. Time is ticking for the man in hiding. He is most wanted for crimes committed. If caught, would lock him away in a cold labor camp for life. If there were only some way to get across that river of death, then his criminal charges would be dropped through international extradition. Moreover, he could also then enjoy the parks, medical care, education, and all the other privileged rights a citizen in that peaceful kingdom enjoys. To this fugitive, nothing matters more than to know how he can get to the other side.

Christ is the drawbridge. "God's grace in Christ is not merely necessary but is the sole efficient cause of salvation. We confess that human beings are born spiritually dead and are incapable even of cooperating with regenerating grace."[11] He is the only way to cross over from the domain of darkness into the kingdom of light. "I AM the gate!" The King of Kings, God's Prince of Peace, is the only passage for man to be positionally moved out from under the curses of sin and death in this world into His holy kingdom of life everlasting. "Truly, I say to you, whoever does not receive the kingdom of God like a child shall not enter it." (Mark 10:15) The way for a sinner to belong in God's kingdom is through Christ alone. "If anyone enters by me, he will be saved." (John 10:9)

---

[11] Alliance of Confessing Evangelicals, *Cambridge Declaration* (1996), Sola Gratia: The Erosion of The Gospel.

God does not contradict His just nature in pardoning sinners and blessing those who deserve the curses of covenant-breaking. "He loves righteousness and justice; the earth is full of the steadfast love of the LORD." (Psalm 33:5) The instrument God uses to declare a cursed sinner blessed is faith in Christ's perfect righteousness that is freely given by God to the believer. "For by grace you have been saved through faith. And this is not your own doing; it is the gift of God." (Ephesians 2:8)

The Christian is reckoned righteous by God when the Spirit unites the believer to Christ. "[A]ll the prophets bear witness that everyone who believes in him receives forgiveness of sins through His name (Acts 10:43) Through Christ's work, the pardoned sinner is brought into a state of "most blessed peace and favor with God and secures every other blessing needful for time and eternity."[12] God promises that "His divine power has granted to us all things that pertain to life and godliness, through the knowledge of him who called us to His own glory." (2 Peter 1:3)

Significance

Every believer and every congregation will face the temptation to act contrary to this belief. Yet, "with the temptation He will also provide the way of escape, that you may be able to endure it." (1 Corinthians 10:13) What I mean is that even if you know that Christ alone is the grounds for your union with God, the next time you sin, Satan will bring into question your standing before God. The Father of Lies accuses,

---

[12] The New Hampshire Confession of Faith (1833), *V.*, Of Justification.

"How could you be really justified since you keep on sinning?" As you understand Christ's work for your justification, you will see more and more why "the accuser of our brothers has been thrown down." (Revelation 12:10)

Another opposite but equally common kink in the Christian's armor is that your fallen flesh will constantly want to creep up as pride in your own strength. "Unwarranted confidence in human ability is a product of fallen human nature."[13] Satan whispers, "No wonder you're justified — you sin so much less than that other man." The Holy Spirit convicts the true believer that such "pride of life—is not from the Father but is from the world." (1 John 2:16)

Within your congregation, you will also feel the pressure at times that your ministry, your faithfulness, or your service must do the heavy lifting for God. As with all blind spots, our pride makes us see it more obviously in others first. "This false confidence now fills the evangelical world," Reformed pastors have observed. "[F]rom the self-esteem gospel, to the health and wealth gospel, from those who have transformed the gospel into a product to be sold and sinners into consumers who want to buy, to others who treat Christian faith as being true simply because it works."[14] God is pleased and glorified when you rest on His word to do all the heavy lifting. God will teach us to trust Christ's word: "'My grace is sufficient for you, for my power is

---

[13] Alliance of Confessing Evangelicals, *Cambridge Declaration* (1996), Sola Gratia.
[14] Alliance of Confessing Evangelicals, *Cambridge Declaration* (1996), Sola Gratia.

made perfect in weakness.' Therefore I will boast all the more gladly of my weaknesses so that the power of Christ may rest upon me." (2 Corinthians 12:9)

Indeed, biblical, Christ-exalting justification comes under attack with fiery arrows from every side. Do you see what's at stake? Man-centered ministry "silences the doctrine of justification regardless of the official commitments of our churches."[15] Wherever God is not exalted in all of man's salvation, there an altogether different, man-centered, Christ-debasing religion exists. "Humble yourselves before the Lord, and He will exalt you." (James 4:10)

I hope that this opening chapter has caused you to see the importance of first becoming and then remaining sharp on the doctrine of justification. Your motive must not be to pick a fight but rather to arm yourself for the war you are already in. "Beloved, do not be surprised at the fiery trial when it comes upon you to test you, as though something strange were happening to you." (1 Peter 4:12) There is far too much at stake. Justification is the great hinge of heaven's gate.

---

[15] Alliance of Confessing Evangelicals, *Cambridge Declaration* (1996), Sola Gratia.

Doxology

I will not boast in anything:
No gifts, no power, no wisdom
But I will boast in Jesus Christ;
His death and resurrection.[16]

Pray through Psalm 24

The earth is the Lord's and the fullness thereof, the world and those who dwell therein,

Who shall ascend the hill of the Lord? And who shall stand in His holy place?

Christ alone has clean hands and a pure heart.
Lift up your heads, O gates! And be lifted up, O ancient doors, that the King of glory may come in. Who is this King of Glory?

The Lord, strong and mighty, the Lord, mighty in battle! Righteousness is from you alone, O God of our salvation.

Make us a generation of those who seek You, who seek Your face, O Triune God. [17]

For Christ's sake, I pray.
Amen.

---

[16] Stuart Townend, *How Deep The Father's Love For Us*, (1996).
[17] Psalm 24.

Chapter 3: The Order of Salvation

The Spine of Grace

Union to Christ is the marrow of true faith. Every truth of our faith is united to Christ at its core. Christ is the "head over all things to the church, which is His body, the fullness of him who fills all in all." (Ephesians 1:22b-23) All doctrines of law and gospel stem from Christ. He is the hub at the center of our religion. Christ is the spine of all saving grace. Yet, our fallen minds which God is still renewing (Romans 12:2) can so easily distort the law and gospel. Therefore, it is vital that our beliefs properly order themselves around Christ.

God created a good and well-ordered cosmos out of nothing, generating time and space into existence by the power of His Word. "God said: 'Let there be light.' God saw that the light was good. And God separated the light from the darkness." (Genesis 1:3-4) In His New Creation, those He redeems by the covenant cut in Christ's blood also take part in His orderly re-creation. In His Church, "all things should be done decently and in order." (1 Corinthians 14:40) God gives His church a structure. His word sequences His great gospel. Since the Middle Ages, the church has called this the *ordo salutis*, which simply means the order of salvation.

In this chapter, my objective is to properly situate the doctrine of justification in logical sequence from God's word. A proper presentation of the gospel as the Bible gives it evokes joy. When you hear it, you feel like the psalmist: "How sweet are your words to my taste, sweeter than honey to my mouth!" (Palm 119:103) Correct biblical order is essential, as I will labor to argue because getting the order wrong will embitter the sweet flavor of the gospel. Notice how perfectly the Holy Spirit, like a master blacksmith, welds together each link of God's gracious salvation chain.

Scripture Text: Romans 8:29-30

29 For those whom He foreknew He also predestined to be conformed to the image of His Son, in order that He might be the firstborn among many brothers. 30 And those whom He predestined He also called, and those whom He called he also justified, and those whom He justified he also glorified.[18]

Context

By the quill of Paul, the Holy Spirit shows us in this glorious chapter of Romans how the Lord Jesus Christ rules from the center of our faith. The order of salvation in these verses unfolds like this: in verse 29, those whom God _____, He also _____.

foreknew — predestined — conformed

God conforms (sanctifies) those He predestined so that Christ might be the firstborn among many brothers. God conforms those who belong to His family. The gospel is God's mission of grace to redeem a people He has loved, the souls of His Bride

---

[18] boldening of words mine.

that He has individually foreknown since before the beginning of time. This wondrous promise is unpacked further in verse 30: those whom God _____, He also _____.

predestined — called — justified — glorified

God chose a people for Himself to conform them to the image of His Son. How does God conform those He predestined? The Bible says that He calls them, justifies them, and prepares them in this present evil age for the glory of the age to come. No blessings exist apart from union with Christ Jesus. Sinners can receive God's saving grace by the ministry of Christ alone as Mediator between God and man. Who are those predestined and foreknown by God? Those whom His Spirit effectually calls and regenerates are the people God will justify. God's elect are struck to the heart to receive justification by God's grace. These are the souls that extend their beggar's hand of faith. Those same believers will grow in Christ's grace. The Holy Spirit will bear His fruit in the lives of God's people until their spiritual union with God consummates in glory.

Doctrine

Those whom God effectually calls He also freely justifies.[19]

---

[19] Second London Baptist Confession of Faith (1677/89), *Chapter 11: Of Justification.*

Significance

Some would say that those who insist on a clear order of salvation are too particular. Here's why it matters, though. Any time a person applies one of the doctrines of grace out of order, they risk distorting God's law and gospel. Law and gospel are for God's glory and man's good. When His truth and love flow through His people, "we carry out this act of grace that is being ministered by us, for the glory of the Lord himself" (2 Corinthians 8:19) When law and gospel are confused, however, we neglect to give God the glory due His name. When law and gospel get distorted, it is never for good.

I'll illustrate what I mean: A man shows up at the emergency room with a visible break above the knee that sends one of his legs mid-thigh in an unnatural direction. The doctor examines the man all over, then sends him home without any treatment, but strongly urges this agonized, if heavy-set patient, to lose 20 lbs. as soon as possible. No one will dispute that the patient could lose a few inches from the midsection. It would even help prevent another bone break in the future if this man could eventually fit into a pair of jeans a couple of sizes smaller. Still, in this case, the E.R. doctor is liable for malpractice. The first treatment that this suffering man needs is to have his femur reset and a strong cast wrapped around his fractured leg. Sadly, such misapplications of biblical truth happen too often when we disrupt the biblical order of salvation, even in our well-meant exhortations to ourselves, to our family members, and within our congregations. Specifically, a person who is not yet justified cannot conform to God's image.

How could the Holy Spirit dwell within and patiently reform a sin-filled nature? How could the just Judge of all commune with a wicked lawbreaker? Who can mediate "between us, who might lay his hand on us both." (Job 9:33)

The Doctrine Opened

God requires first that His justice be satisfied. "I will not acquit the wicked." (Exodus 23:7). Therefore, the claims of His justice must be paid in full, either by ourselves or another.[20] "He will render to each one according to his works." (Romans 2:6) According to God's righteous judgment, we deserve punishment both in this world and forever after: how can we escape this punishment and return to God's favor?[21]

Telling an unregenerated, unrepentant sinner to fulfill the Ten Commandments by his fleshly strength is like ordering the obese ER patient to limp upon his shattered femur 50 miles per day until he sheds a few pounds. The order of salvation matters for life in Christ and ministry. To be less than "particular" on the order of salvation is to commit spiritual malpractice. God holds such negligence accountable: "The sick you have not healed, the injured you have not bound up." (Ezekiel 34:4)

When a person feels the weight of God's law, their first step of obedience is not to work harder at being a good person but to trust in Christ the Savior. "I will put my trust in him." (Hebrews 2:13) To urge an unconverted sinner to bear the fruit of the Spirit is

---

[20] Hercules Collins, *An Orthodox Catechism* (1660), Q:12.
[21] Hercules Collins, *An Orthodox Catechism* (1660), Q:12.

to push man-centered moralism upon him. "For no good tree bears bad fruit, nor again does a bad tree bear good fruit." (Luke 6:43)

The logical connection between each doctrine of grace in sequence is also important to combat the waves of doubt that swell up seasonally in the mind of every believer, threatening to shipwreck our faith. It was God who gave you a mind to think. It is God who embedded laws to govern His created realm. Logical sequence is a gift of God's "mercy on those who doubt." (Jude 1:22) If you've ever doubted your election, there is a remedy. The order of salvation helps strengthen assurance. Let me summarize this remedy by drawing from the clear thought of a Puritan minister.

To keep the biblical doctrines of grace ordered within the structure God has given in the Bible, an early Puritan pastor named William Perkins (1558–1602) wrote a book called A Golden Chain in 1590.[22] In this book, he provides a visual organizer of the flow between each act of God in bringing His people to heaven. At the heart of Perkin's visual organizer is the work of Jesus Christ – the mediator between God and man. Perkins insisted that every doctrine of grace was bound to Christ.

The flow of salvific grace begins with God the Father choosing the elect in Christ. God "chose us in him before the foundation of the world." (Ephesians 1:4) When they hear God's effectual call, they repent of sin and trust in Christ. "[W]hen the Gentiles heard

---

[22] Perkins, William. *The Works of William Perkins, Volume 1*. Reformation Heritage Books, 2014.

this, they began rejoicing and glorifying the word of the Lord, and as many as were appointed to eternal life believed." (Acts 13:48)

The wounds of Christ have paid the ransom of all His elect. For "the Son of Man came not to be served but to serve, and to give His life as a ransom for many." (Mark 10:45) Christ extends the blessings He gained from His reward to His elect. Through Christ's work, His people from every people, nation, tribe, and tongue "have come to share in their spiritual blessings." (Romans 15:27) Not only are they justified, but the elect also are then conformed to the image of Christ. "[T]hose whom He foreknew He also predestined to be conformed to the image of His Son. (Romans 8:39) In Christ, God will raise you to glory. "[H]e who raised the Lord Jesus will raise us also with Jesus and bring us with you into His presence." (2 Corinthians 4:14) Oh, how blessed to be among His ransomed people!

Still, how do you know whether you are truly among them? Doctor Perkins correctly applied the medicine of justification to the temptation every new Christian will face to doubt your election. If you ever wonder whether you are among God's elect, God's word compassionately reminds us to repent of sin and believe in Jesus Christ once again. "Out of the anguish of His soul He shall see and be satisfied; by His knowledge shall the righteous one, my servant, make many to be accounted righteous, and He shall bear their iniquities." (Isaiah 53:11) When you put in the labor to work out the logic of the order of your salvation in Christ, you are applying Christ's medicine to your soul.

Trust that Jesus bore your iniquities. "[U]pon him was the chastisement that brought us peace." (Isaiah 53:5) Because of His righteousness, God has accounted you righteous in Christ. (Romans 4:3) Your ongoing trust in Christ alone for your salvation confirms that you are justified. "May the God of hope fill you with all joy and peace in believing, so that by the power of the Holy Spirit you may abound in hope." (Romans 15:13)

You whom God has justified, He also will glorify, because it is you that He foreknew and predestined to be united to Christ. Because you are united with Christ, the Spirit will bear fruit in your life, growing you in conformity to His Son until you are properly re-ordered, re-created, and re-formed. "Whoever abides in me and I in Him, he it is that bears much fruit, for apart from me you can do nothing." (John 15:5) As this happens, enjoy the comfort that God predestined you to be part of His new creation – spiritually now, soon consummately, and after that, forevermore. Union to Christ is the heart of true religion. Every doctrine in our *ordo salutis* depends upon the union of the elect to Christ.

Doxology

Why should I gain from His reward?
I cannot give an answer,

But this I know with all my heart:
his wounds have paid my ransom.[23]

Pray through Romans 8:3-4

O gracious God!

You have done what no sinner, condemned under

Your moral law and weakened by the flesh, could do.

You sent Your own Son in the likeness of sinful flesh
to pay the curse of my sin.

In Christ's flesh, you condemned my sin in order that
the righteous requirement of the law might be fulfilled
in us.

Train us to walk not according to our flesh but
according to Your Spirit. [24]

For Christ's sake, I pray.
Amen.

---

[23] Stuart Townend, *How Deep The Father's Love For Us,* (1996).
[24] Romans 8:3-4.

Chapter 4: Criminals Who Plead Guilty

Who does God justify?

So far, my goal has been to wave the banner of this foundational truth: *Justification is by grace alone through faith alone because of Christ alone.* Justification is the truth upon which the church stands or falls. Sadly, this truth is often downplayed, distorted, or sometimes even denied by leaders, scholars, and pastors who claim to be evangelical.[25] The Bible's robust teaching on justification can be neglected or distorted most when it comes to the question: "Who does God justify?"

Specifically, when we, the Church, are not clear about who receives the blessings of the covenant of grace and who remains under the covenant of works, we fail. "For land that has drunk the rain that often falls on it, and produces a crop useful to those for whose sake it is cultivated, receives a blessing from God. But if it bears thorns and thistles, it is worthless and near to being cursed, and its end is to be burned." (Hebrews 6:7-8)

---

[25] Alliance of Confessing Evangelicals, *Cambridge Declaration* (1996), Sola Fide.

Scripture Text: **Romans 5:17–19**

17 For if, because of one man's trespass, death reigned through that one man, much more will those who receive the abundance of grace and the free gift of righteousness reign in life through the one man Jesus Christ. 18 Therefore, as one trespass led to condemnation for all men, so one act of righteousness leads to justification and life for all men. 19 For as by the one man's disobedience the many were made sinners, so by the one man's obedience the many will be made righteous.

Context

In this passage, Paul shows the principle by which all are under the condemnation of sin because of the federal headship of Adam. That is, since in Adam's sin, all of his race inherits the curse of the fall and death reigns over their lives. Sin pollutes every deed of man. The trespass of Adam has put all of mankind under condemnation before the Holy Triune God.

Yet, this stark message of condemnation serves as the dark backdrop upon which the gospel glimmers brightly in the foreground. "For as by the one man's disobedience the many were made sinners, so by the one man's obedience the many will be made righteous." (Romans 5:19) By this same principle, cursed sinners can have hope if a second federal head can fulfill the work that is necessary to secure life for a multitude. "Behold, the days are coming, declares the LORD, when I will make a new covenant…"

(Jeremiah 31:31)

All are born into sin. Every intention of our hearts corrupts every one of our actions, bringing us into further and further condemnation. "[T]he law came in to increase the trespass." (Romans 5:20) We are criminals whom our Creator will not pardon until we plead guilty to the charges against us.

Doctrine

God is satisfied to pardon His people by Christ's death in their place.[26]

Significance

To leave an unrepentant sinner living in the superficial comfort of a false assurance of salvation is to act in an unloving way toward that person. It is irresponsible and unsympathetic when ambassadors of the Just Judge misrepresent the terms of pardon. "Rather, speaking the truth in love, we are to grow up in every way into him who is the head, into Christ" (Ephesians 4:15) It will be a shock for spiritual criminals who continue to plead themselves "not guilty" on the Lord's final day of reckoning. "Not everyone who says to me, 'Lord, Lord,' will enter the kingdom of heaven ... I declare to them, 'I never knew you; depart from me, you workers of lawlessness." (Matthew 7:21, 23) Before any blessings of justification can be enjoyed, spiritual

---

[26] Second London Baptist Confession of Faith (1677/89), *Chapter 11: Of Justification.*

criminals must plead guilty before God.

Many career ministers fear losing their jobs if they were to look those who give financial support to their church in the eye and declare in plain terms: "If you do not repent, none of God's promises are for you. You remain under the curse of sin. You are a criminal in need of pardon. If you do not plead guilty before God, you perish." God says of such false shepherds: "They have healed the wound of my people lightly, saying, 'Peace, peace,' when there is no peace." (Jeremiah 6:14)

The Doctrine Opened
So, whom does God justify? Our just God justifies all those whom He effectually calls. Those who hear the voice of the Holy Shepherd-King melt in the heart at the sight of the Savior. "My sheep hear my voice, and I know them, and they follow me." (John 10:27). They confess their sins against Him and plead for His pardon by grace alone. If you have experienced the effectual call of God, you know what it is to tremble under the holiness of God, to weep at the offense of your sin before Him, to behold His love in Christ "for a sinner such as I." Those whom God justifies respond as an inmate on death row who receives the king's pardon:

> *My terrors all vanished before the sweet name;*
> *My guilty fears banished, with boldness I came*
> *To drink at the fountain, life-giving and free*

Jehovah Tsidkenu (Lord, my righteousness) is all things to me.[27]

Consider the cost Christ paid to cancel your debt so that you might freely live. "I lay down my life for the sheep." (John 10:15) This truth is illustrated in this gut-wrenching event that Alaskan pastors retell.[28] Every night, the ocean tide rises, flooding the sandy banks at the dock in Anchorage, Alaska. The daytime tide is low, exposing the banks, but all the locals know not to walk out on the soft, water-saturated sand. However, one day, two vacationing teenage brothers visited the city and strolled onto the wet, sandy banks. As the younger brother ventured closer to the fierce Pacific breakers, first his shoes, then his calves, and soon his knees were swallowed up by the sinking sand. His older brother ran out to help him. Soon, however, both brothers were buried alive up to their armpits in the sandy water.

By the time a helicopter rescue patrolman dangled above their death trap, only one outstretched arm was visible. The boy was lifted into the helicopter, but when asked about his brother, he gasped through tears: "He's gone." "How do you know?" the rescuers demanded three times. Finally able to spit out the words, amid his shock: "I know my brother is dead because he made me stand on his shoulders."

---

[27] Robert Murray M'Cheyne, *Jehovah Tsidkenu,* (1867).
[28] I heard a version of this illustration in a sermon by Pastor Asher Griffin of Crosspoint Church in Enid, OK.

The Lord Jesus Christ, who calls you His brother,[29] made himself low to the point of death and burial in your place so that you could stand upon Him and live. "What benefits do they that are effectually called partake of in this life? They that are effectually called do in this life partake of justification, adoption, sanctification, and the several benefits which in this life do either accompany or flow from them."[30]

Doxology

My hope is built on nothing less
Than Jesus' blood and righteousness.
I dare not trust the sweetest frame
But wholly lean on Jesus' name.
On Christ, the solid rock I stand,
All other ground is sinking sand.[31]

Pray through Psalm 32:1-5

O Lord, when I kept silent, my bones wasted away through my groaning all day long.

All day and all night, your hand was heavy upon me; my strength was dried up as by the heat of summer. But now, Lord, I acknowledge my sin to you. I do not cover my iniquity. I confess my transgressions to the Lord.

---

[29] Hebrews 2:11–12 "He is not ashamed to call them brothers, saying, 'I will declare your name to my brothers."

[30] Benjamin Keach's Catechism (1666), Q. 36. See also Rom. 8:30; Gal. 3:26; 1 Cor. 6:11; Rom. 8:31-32; Eph. 1:5; 1 Cor. 1:30.

[31] Edwards Mote, *My Hope Is Built On Nothing Less,* (1867).

You forgave the iniquity of my sin. O my sin, most offensive and vile.

Now I know this is true: Blessed is the one whose transgression is forgiven, whose sin is covered.

Blessed is the man against whom the Lord counts no iniquity and in whose spirit there is no deceit. [32]

For Christ's sake, I pray.
Amen.

---

[32] Psalm 32:1-5.

Chapter 5: The Necessary Work of the Son

Hell-Deserving Deficiencies

Man is born with two hell-deserving deficiencies. First, man's sin deserves death. "[T]he wages of sin is death." (Romans 6:23) "God's justice demands that [sinful man] must pay for [his] sin, but [one] sinner could never pay for others."[33] Second, even if God were to simply pardon sinners all of their transgressions, man still lacks the righteousness that the Holy God requires for eternal life. "None is righteous, no, not one." (Romans 3:10) Man is "by nature utterly void of that holiness required by the law of God." What makes man's black station even darker is that man is "positively inclined to evil."[34] Left on this earth to ourselves, we are all defenseless, hopeless, and excuseless. "So they are without excuse." (Romans 1:20) Unless God Himself saves,

all shall perish. "Salvation belongs to the LORD!" (Jonah 2:9)

---

[33] An Orthodox Catechism – Question 16, citing Rom. 5:12, 15; 1 Cor. 15:21; Heb. 2:14–16 (b) Heb. 7:26-27; 1 Pet. 3:18.

[34] In context, the full paragraph states: *"We believe that man was created in holiness, under the law of his Maker; but by voluntary transgression fell from that holy and happy state; in consequence of which all mankind are now sinners, not by constraint, but choice; being by nature utterly void of that holiness required by the law of God, positively inclined to evil; and therefore under just condemnation to eternal ruin, without defense or excuse."* The New Hampshire Confession of Faith (1833), Article III, Of the Fall of Man.

Scripture Text: **1 Peter 1:18–19**

[K]nowing that you were ransomed from the futile ways inherited from your forefathers, not with perishable things such as silver or gold, but with the precious blood of Christ, like that of a lamb without blemish or spot.

Doctrine

God justifies sinners by imputing Christ's active obedience unto the whole law.[35]

Context

Adam's heirs owe God an unpayable debt. Man is impoverished. There is nothing man can offer to God as a contribution to pay for his ransom. Even if man offers up his own life, it is too full of sin and blemishes to be of any value. Could anything in the life of a mortal merit anything to pay a debt owed to an eternal God? If God does not act, man will perish in his way. "[T]he way of the wicked will perish." (Psalm 1:6) Notice how scripture describes Christ's work to save God's people.

Because of sin, each of us is under God's just condemnation unto eternal ruin. "Whoever does not obey the Son shall not see life, but the wrath of God remains on him." (John 3:36) It's as if Peter is preaching to the Church: "See your necessity of Christ's work on your behalf! Think of the path you

---

[35] Second London Baptist Confession of Faith (1677/89), *Chapter 11: Of Justification.*

were on under the curse of sin. Ponder your complete poverty — you had absolutely no way to pay for your own ransom. You were doomed to remain a slave to sin, Satan, and the world for life. You were hopeless to come up with anything from this perishing world that could satisfy the justice of the eternal God." The point of this passage is that man needs God Himself to act.

The Doctrine Opened

It was necessary to save sinners that God's only begotten Son become the final Adam[36] — the firstborn of the new creation.[37] God's holiness and justice demand the work of a Mediator. The Mediator must be able to save man from both of his hell-deserving deficiencies. "[T]here is one mediator between God and men, the man Christ Jesus" (1 Timothy 2:5)

First, because our sin deserves death, the Mediator must be truly human to die as a substitute in the place of sinful man. "By this we know love, that He laid down His life for us." (1 John 3:16) It is necessary for our salvation that Jesus Christ, the Creator who took on flesh for His Bride, "sustained in body and soul the anger of God against the sin of the whole human race. This He did in order that, by His suffering as the only atoning sacrifice, He might set us free, body and soul, from eternal condemnation."[38]

---

[36] 1 Corinthians 15:45 "The first man Adam became a living being"; the last Adam became a life-giving spirit."
[37] 2 Corinthians 5:17 "Therefore, if anyone is in Christ, he is a new creation. The old has passed away; behold, the new has come."
[38] Collins, *An Orthodox Catechism*, Question 37.

Second, because pardoned sinners still cannot merit eternal life, the Mediator must be truly righteous to fulfill God's holy requirement. "For our sake He made him to be sin who knew no sin, so that in him we might become the righteousness of God." (2 Corinthians 5:21) It is necessary for our salvation that Jesus Christ, the only Mediator between God and man, who Himself lacked nothing, actively obeyed His Father to fulfill the righteousness we lack. It required the blood of God's Son whose life proved Him to be perfect, as "a lamb without blemish or spot." (1 Peter 1:19) It was necessary: "That during His whole life on earth," Christ would live blamelessly, perfectly loving God and neighbor, "gain for us God's grace, righteousness, and eternal life."[39]

Let me illustrate it like this. There lies the handicapped middle-aged man unable to sleep. He knows that at any moment, the legendary blade of one of the new king's mighty men may slice his neck open. He inherited a death sentence from his forefather. The paraplegic's grandfather had been obsessed with destroying the exiled general who has now claimed the throne. Because of his paralysis, he cannot run away or even work to sustain himself. He is completely enslaved without any hope of achieving freedom for himself. This story we read of in 2 Samuel.

In 2 Samuel 9:1, David asks the Jerusalem courtiers: "Is there still anyone left of the house of Saul, that I may show him kindness for Jonathan's sake?" In David's eyes, Jonathan earned blessings for

---

[39] Collins, *An Orthodox Catechism*, Question 37.

the rest of his line. Mephibosheth was cursed as a son of Saul, but he was ransomed by the powerful king out of love for the selfless, sacrificial life and death of the noble prince Jonathan. For Mephibosheth, Jonathan's blessings surpassed Saul's sin.

Oh, believer, you and I are Mephibosheth! Our Saul is Adam, but our Jonathan is Christ. Just as David showed covenant commitment to Mephibosheth for Jonathan's sake, so God shows you and me His glorious kindness for Christ's sake. See the "immeasurable riches of His grace and kindness toward us in Christ Jesus." (Ephesians 2:7)

God's word reminds you, Christian, to: "See your need of Christ's work on your behalf! Christ alone can provide all you need. His righteousness alone is unblemished. His life alone had not spot. His blood alone is pure." Oh believer, rest in God's promise that "your sins are forgiven for His name's sake." (1 John 2:12) Praise God that "Christ, by His obedience, and death, did fully discharge the debt of all those that are justified; and did by the sacrifice of himself, in the blood of His cross, undergoing in their stead, the penalty due unto them: make a proper, real and full satisfaction to God's justice in their behalf."[40] His sacrifice alone God accepts. His payment alone is imperishable. Christ's ransom alone makes you belong to God. "Who will not fear, O Lord, and glorify your name? For you alone are holy. All nations will come and worship you, for your righteous acts have been revealed." (Revelation 15:4)

---

[40] 2LCF 11:3.

Significance

Martin Luther gave this counsel to a former student of his: "When the devil throws our sins up to us and declares that we deserve death and hell, we ought to speak thus: 'I admit that I deserve death and hell. What of it? Does this mean that I shall be sentenced to eternal damnation? By no means. For I know One who suffered and made satisfaction on my behalf. His name is Jesus Christ, Son of God, and where He is there I shall be also.'"[41]

Doxology

Praise God from Whom all blessings flow!

Your perfect Law exposes me.
I feel my sin and desperate need.
My best good works are powerless
To satisfy Your righteousness.
But there is One who lived for me,
His life, my only victory.
His death forever sealed in time,
That I am His and He is mine.

Praise God from Whom all blessings flow!
Praise Him, all creatures here below.
Praise Him above, ye heavenly hosts.
Praise Father, Son, and Holy Ghost.[42]

---

[41] Luther, Martin. *Luther: Letters of Spiritual Counsel*. Vol. 18. Regent College Publishing, 2003.

Pray

I praise you, My Three-In-One God!
Salvation cannot be found in anyone else.

You, My Lord Jesus Christ, are my only high priest
who has set us free by the one sacrifice of His body.

You, My Lord Jesus Christ, continually plead my
cause with the Father.

You, My Lord Jesus Christ, are my eternal king.
You govern us by Your word and Spirit.

You, My Lord Jesus Christ, guard me and keep me
free from sin because I belong to you now.

To You be all glory, honor, and praise, now and
forevermore.[43]

For Christ's sake, I pray.
Amen.

---

[42] Lyrics by Zach Hicks and Thomas Ken, *The Gospel Doxology* (1637).
[43] adapted from Hercules Collins, *An Orthodox Catechism, Questions 29-30,* (1680).

Chapter 6: For the Glory of God

Can You Behold God's Glory?

"God is Spirit." (John 4:24) So, how can you and I
behold His glory? God is infinite, eternal, and
unchangeable in His being, wisdom, power, holiness,
justice, goodness, and truth.[44] How can fallen,
depraved creatures who are blinded by sin behold
God's attributes? "We shall surely die, for we have
seen God." (Judges 13:12) This, God accomplished
by the work of Christ in justification.

God defuses His glory into the world He
created. To behold with the eyes of faith any one
aspect of God's essence is to behold His glory more
deeply. "Behold, the LORD our God has shown us His
glory and greatness." (Deuteronomy 5:24) In the text
below, Paul strings together a series of pearls to
answer the question of how justification allows you to
behold God's glory.

Scriptural Focus: **Ephesians 1:6-7**

*To the praise of the glory of His grace, wherein He
has made us accepted in the beloved. In whom we
have redemption through His blood, the forgiveness of
sins, according to the riches of His grace.*

---

[44] Benjamin Keach's Catechism (1666), Q. 8. See also John 4:24; Ps. 147:5; Ps.
90:2; James 1:17; Rev. 4:8; Ps. 89:14; Exod. 34:6-7; 1 Tim. 1:17.

Context

Paul writes to the church in Ephesus that those who were once spiritually dead, condemned, and rejected in the vileness of their sin are now accepted by God. How can this be possible? They are accepted in God's Beloved, in union with the heavenly Father's only begotten Son.

How can slaves to sin be united to God the Son? God's word says: "We have redemption through His blood." (Ephesians 1:7) How does Christ redeem? On the cross of Calvary, God The Son paid the full price and took the entire punishment that your sin deserves. "You are completely clean" (John 13:10) His blood purchased your redemption. He paid your complete debt so that you can live at peace, trusting His finished work, fully accomplishing for you "the forgiveness of sins."

Doctrine

The Father is glorified in the Son's justifying work.[45]

The Doctrine Opened

Anyone who has ears to hear this glorious gospel message will next ponder the inevitable questions: Why? How can this be? To what end? In other words, can we know why God justifies sinners? In this text, the gospel promises are bookended by the answer to this question. God justifies sinners "[t]o the praise of the glory of His grace ... according to the riches of

---

[45] Second London Baptist Confession of Faith (1677/89), *Chapter 11: Of Justification.*

His grace." (Ephesians 1:6-7)

God's justification of sinners by the work of Christ reveals both God's justice and God's grace to creation. God is both just and gracious. "It was the will of God, that Christ by the blood of the cross, whereby He confirmed the new covenant, should effectually redeem out of every people, tribe, nation, and language, all those, and those only, who were from eternity chosen to salvation and given to Him by the Father."[46] God justifies sinners because of who He is.

Significance

Through the work of Christ, believers can behold the glory of the Father. "[W]e have seen His glory, glory as of the only Son from the Father, full of grace and truth." (John 1:14) See the glory of the Father in accepting Christ's obedience in your place. "No one takes it from me, but I lay it down of my own accord. I have authority to lay it down, and I have authority to take it up again. This charge I have received from my Father." (John 10:18)

See the glory of the Father in being satisfied by Christ's atonement in your stead. "To declare ... His righteousness: that He might be just, and the justifier of him which believeth in Jesus." (Romans 3:26, KJV) Your justification by God's free grace magnifies God's glory. In saving sinners by free grace alone the "exact justice and rich grace of God" are magnified. The gospel is so clearly for man's good

---

[46] Alliance of Confessing Evangelicals, *Cambridge Declaration* (1996), Sola Fide.

and so that God "might be glorified in the Justification of sinners."[47]

Justification reveals the glory of God by magnifying His exact justice. Question 10 of *An Orthodox Catechism* asks: "Will God permit such disobedience and rebellion to go unpunished?" The biblical answer is clear: "Certainly not. He is terribly angry about the sin we are born with as well as the sins we personally commit. As a just judge, He punishes them now and in eternity."[48] Because God is just, He is glorified by punishing everyone who sins against Him. He must fulfill what He revealed: "Cursed is everyone who does not continue to do everything written in the Book of the Law." (Deuteronomy 27:26) God fulfills His exact justice by putting every single one of the sins of His people upon His Son's back on the cross and dying the death that the just God requires of law-breakers. "Great and amazing are your deeds, O Lord God the Almighty! Just and true are your ways, O King of the nations!" (Revelation 15:3)

Justification reveals the glory of God by magnifying His rich grace. "For God has not destined us for wrath, but for obtaining salvation through our Lord Jesus Christ." (1 Thessalonians 5:9) The richness of God's grace is proved by the richness of Christ's blood. 1 John 2:2. "He [Christ] Himself is the propitiation for our sins." Christ's rich blood satisfied the justice of God. "He Himself bore our sins in His body on the tree." (1 Peter 2:24) The torturous, substitutionary end of Christ's rich life appeased

[47] 2LCF 11.3.
[48] An Orthodox Catechism (1680), Q10.

divine wrath against sin. God lavishes His rich grace forgiving the sins of His people by the penal substitutionary atonement of His only begotten Son on behalf of law-breakers. "In him we have redemption through His blood, the forgiveness of our trespasses, according to the riches of His grace, which He lavished upon us." (Ephesians 1:7-8)

Christians know that salvation is by God's free grace, not by their own works. However, all Christians can be easily deceived to think that our perseverance in the faith depends on our own works. To put it another way, you will give God all the glory in your justification. Still, you will be tempted to siphon off some of His glory for yourself in your sanctification. Christ is "he who sanctifies." (Hebrews 2:11)

Serious error in confusing law with gospel on this doctrine has caused many believers to despair. Contemplate, for example, an already tired mother of three little ones under six who only gets four hours of sleep each night. "I'm so confused now," she mumbles to herself as she brushes her teeth before getting the kids up for another full day. She thinks to herself, "that pastor said that God's grace will be there only 'for those who keep the covenant.' There is no way I can keep God's covenant. I must not be in His covenant. Maybe I've never had God's grace."[49]

---

[49] Even our well-respected brother John Piper may have confused law and gospel in this quotation: "When the Old Testament says that covenant keeping is the condition for receiving God's loving kindness, that's what it meant ... All the covenants of God are conditional covenants of grace-both the old and the new covenant. They offer all sufficient Future Grace for those who keep the covenant. But what it does say is that all future blessings of the Christian life are conditional on our keeping." Future Grace pg. 249

This poor (though relatable) mother needs to hear the gospel untainted. She needs to hear the truth that God will preserve her in the faith. God will do this not as a fruit of her good works but as "a fruit of election." God will preserve her in the faith not because she meets the conditional terms of perfect, personal, and perpetual obedience that none can keep, but as "a gift of God gained by the death of Christ"[50] She needs to be reminded that the same God who justified her by faith will produce good works in her. For "we are not of those who shrink back and are destroyed, but of those who have faith and preserve their souls." (Hebrews 10:39) She is justified by faith upon one condition: Christ's work, not her own. She will be sanctified, preserved, and finally saved into the age to come by this and no other condition: by Christ's work, not her own. "He preserves the lives of His saints." (Psalm 97:10)

This glorious gospel of God's rich grace also leads us to trust in God's goodness. "[H]e hath made him [to be] sin for us, who knew no sin; that we might be made the righteousness of God in him." (2 Corinthians 5:21) Hear how Paul applied the gospel of justification in this way. He wrote: "He that spared not His own Son, but delivered him up for us all, how shall He not with him also freely give us all things?" (Romans 8:32) When Satan tempts you to doubt the richness of God's grace, remember that God "spared not His own Son" to save you. When the remaining sin of your flesh deceives you into feeling that you

---

[50] "For the Holy Scripture testifies that this follows out of election and is given the elect in virtue of the death, the resurrection and intercession of Christ." Cannons of Dort, Fifth Head of Doctrine

merit God's favor, remember that the same God who "delivered up" His own Son freely will "freely give us all things." The promise of God's rich grace is only for you who receive it freely.

If you are living under a principle of works to merit God's favor, you are robbing God of His glory. His grace is not for you. "But to the one who does not work, but believes in Him who justifies the ungodly, his faith is reckoned as righteousness." (Romans 4:5) He who saved you will preserve you. "That in the ages to come He might show the exceeding riches of His grace in [his] kindness toward us through Christ Jesus." (Ephesians 2:7) You are saved for God's glory alone. God will sanctify you for His glory alone. God will preserve you for His glory alone. Do not let your heart be troubled. Instead, rejoice you are saved for the glory of God!

Doxology

Till on that cross as Jesus died,
The wrath of God was satisfied
For every sin on Him was laid;
Here in the death of Christ, I live. [51]

Pray

O Lord! Your steadfast love never ends!
In saving, You also have justified me,
Accounting me righteous by Your own decree,

Declaring me guiltless of all of my sin,
And bringing Your wrath against me to an end.

This wrath Christ appeased in full brunt on the Tree,
When, bearing my sin, He endured it for me.[52]

Thank you, Lord, that your steadfast love never ends!
Your mercies are new every morning.
Great is Your faithfulness, O Lord![53]

For Christ's sake, I pray.
Amen.

---

[51] Keith & Kristyn Getty, "In Christ Alone," (2001).
[52] Milton Vincent, *A Gospel Primer: For Christians*, p. 73-74.
[53] See Lamentations 3:22-23.

Chapter 7: Live in Christ's Righteous Merits

Your Double Imputation

A brief review at this point may be helpful. Imputation means that what belongs to one person is put onto another. What was imputed in your salvation? The Bible teaches that Christ's work includes not one but two different imputations for His people, both of which are necessary for your salvation.

First, Christ made your death sentence His own. The punishment you deserved was put on Christ as your substitute. He bore the wrath of God in His body on the cross in your place. Praise God for this first imputation. Second, Christ made His perfect righteousness your own. "He justifies sinners by imputing Christ's active obedience unto the whole law."[54] Praise God for His double imputation in justifying you.

Yet, how often do you and I struggle to live in the reality of Christ's double imputation? Those God justifies and calls righteous do not then start living by their own strength of the flesh. "The righteous shall live by faith." (Romans 1:17)

This chapter aims to exhort you. If you are justified, you now live in Christ's righteousness. His merits are yours. God has made His holiness your

---

[54] Second London Baptist Confession of Faith (1677/89), *Chapter 11: Of Justification.*

own. This changes everything about how you live. John Angell James (1785–1859) wrote, "Before justification, we have no right to joy; and after it no reason for misery." [55] The goodness of God is the fuel of your life. "[T]he joy of the LORD is your strength." (Nehemiah 8:10)

Scripture Text: John 1:12

But as many as received him, to them He gave power to become the sons of God, [even] to them that believe on His name.

Context

John sets up the fourth Gospel, urging Christians to believe in Christ. In this verse, God's word teaches that to believe in Christ's name is to receive the power of Christ to live as a child of God. This is remarkable for numerous reasons. Your bondage to sin under Adam's curse is removed. You receive from Christ the power to become children of God. "For if by one man's offense, death reigned by one; much more they which receive abundance of grace and of the gift of righteousness shall reign in life by one, Jesus Christ." (Romans 5:17)

This means that you are not in slavery to live under the torment of Satan, the Father of Lies. (John 8:44) Rather, Christ's power, the same power that crushed the devil's head, fills you, grows you, and matures in you whom He saved. "[S]o that we may no longer be children, tossed to and for by the waves and

---

[55] James, John Angell. *The anxious inquirer after salvation directed and encouraged.* No. 61. Religious Tract Society, (1880).

carried about by every wind of doctrine." (Ephesians 4:14) The Spirit caused you to believe in Christ's name. The Spirit regenerated you to receive Christ as your Lord and Savior. "The Lord opened [your] heart to pay attention to what was said." (Acts 16:14) This same Spirit trains you to live as a child of God, "according to the foreknowledge of God the Father, in the sanctification of the Spirit, for obedience to Jesus Christ." (1 Peter 1:2)

Doctrine

Live according to the truth that God counts Christ's righteous merits as your own.[56]

The Doctrine Opened

Christ's gospel is under fire not only in justification but also in what we teach about Christian living. "[F]allen human nature has always recoiled from recognizing its need for Christ's imputed righteousness."[57] The exhortation to live in truth that Christ's righteousness is your own has the potential to become distorted. Satan loves to twist any aspect of the gospel. Lucifer's motive in doing this is to try to dim the glory of Christ in this present evil age. "Are we to continue in sin that grace may abound? By no means! How can we who died to sin still live in it?" (Romans 6:1-2)

One such dangerous distortion is this teaching:

---

[56] Second London Baptist Confession of Faith (1677/89), *Chapter 11: Of Justification.*

[57] Alliance of Confessing Evangelicals, *Cambridge Declaration* (1996), Sola Fide.

that how you live is a condition for your justification. In other words, it would mean that you are not fully justified until you prove it by your living. This would mean that you must live as a Christian under a principle of works. This would mean that your salvation is contingent upon your law-keeping. This is to say that you get some of the glory in your justification. This would mean that how you live can jeopardize your justification. This would mean that Christ did not fully save you, that He did not completely justify you. This is a dangerous lie. It is only those who realize none but God are worthy to have a place around His heavenly throne. "Worthy are you, our Lord and God, to receive glory and honor and power." (Revelation 4:11)

Our good news is that Christ's double imputation addresses these distortions. "Is there injustice on God's part? By no means!" (Romans 9:14) God commits no injustice by requiring in His law what no man is capable of doing. "God created humans with the ability to keep the law. They, however, tempted by the devil, in reckless disobedience, robbed themselves and all their descendants of these gifts."[58] Yet, God did not lower His standard. "But you, you are to be feared! Who can stand before you when once your anger is roused?" (Psalm 67:7) God's perfect holiness suffers no loss by man's sin.

Instead, God took on flesh to fulfill the law Himself. "I am the LORD, your Holy One, the Creator

---

[58] An Orthodox Catechism, Q. 9.

of Israel, your King." (Isaiah 43:15) He then fully imputes His complete righteousness on those He justifies. "Behold, I have taken your iniquity away from you, and I will clothe you with pure vestments." (Zechariah 3:4) God paid out the full wages of death that sinners deserve on His own Son who hung on the cursed tree in their place. "Being justified freely by His grace through the redemption that is in Christ Jesus: whom God hath set forth to be a propitiation through faith in His blood" (Rom. 3:24–25).[59] How you live adds nothing to accomplish your salvation. If you are saved, then you are saved fully, completely, entirely by God alone.

So now God relates to me only with grace
The former wrath banished without any trace!
And each day I'm made a bit more as I should,
His grace using all things to render me good.
Yes, even in trials God's grace abounds too
And does me the good He assigns it to do.[60]

Significance
Due to the curse of sin, "Christ had to go all the way to death because God's justice and truth demand it: only the death of God's Son could pay for our sin."[61] Since Christ's obedience, even to the point of death on a cross, accomplished your salvation, you live in the freedom that you contribute nothing to your

[59] Cannons of Dort, Second Head of Doctrine. Rejection 4.
[60] Milton Vincent, *A Gospel Primer: For Christians*, p. 74.
[61] An Orthodox Catechism, Q. 40.

salvation. You live this way by "looking to Jesus, the founder and perfecter of our faith, who for the joy that was set before him endured the cross, despising the shame, and is seated at the right hand of the throne of God." (Hebrews 12:2) Look to Jesus and live a life of gratitude and assurance, which are His entirely free gifts to you.

Your life is a house. A good house is peaceful. It is free of fear. It is warmed by unconditional love. If your house is built upon the foundation of your own merits, you live within it tormented by constant anxiety. You will not be able to enjoy a sunny day because you'll fear the destruction that the smallest cloud could bring. Your own merits are shifting sand and lack a reliable foundation. Jesus warns you: "[E]veryone who hears these words of mine and does not do them will be like a foolish man who built his house on the sand." (Matthew 7:25)

By contrast, when your life is built upon the Rock of Ages, there is no storm in life that it cannot withstand. (Matthew 7:24-26) The only way to live in peace, free of fear, and with a secure standing in God is to live your life fully resting on Christ's righteous merits. Jesus invites you: "[L]earn from me, for I am gentle and lowly in heart, and you will find rest for your souls." (Matthew 11:29) When you grasp your security in God's covenant bond, which He promised, accomplished, and applied to you, the way you live changes. If you are grafted into Christ, the True Vine (John 15:1), then to you "belong the adoption, the glory, the covenants, the giving of the law, the worship, and the promises." (Romans 9:4) You realize that to put any hope in your own merits is like building a home upon sinking sands. Instead, you trust in the solid rock of Christ alone. Then and only then is your life secure!

> *His oath, His covenant, His blood*
> *Support me in the whelming flood*
> *When all around my soul gives way*
> *He then is all my hope and stay*[62]

God makes Christ's righteousness your own by pardoning your sins, by accounting and accepting to you His righteousness. God justifies you freely, fully, and finally for Christ's sake alone by imputing Christ's active obedience unto the whole law upon you. God made your sentence Christ's own by His passive obedience in His death. So now, you enjoy Christ's sole and whole righteousness. How? By receiving and resting on Christ. Trust God's promise that His righteousness is accounted as yours by faith. "[T]o the one who does not work but believes in him who justifies the ungodly, his faith is counted as righteousness." (Romans 4:5) Relax further in the assurance that even your faith is not of your own doing, it is the gift of God. (Ephesians 2:8)

Do you want a life marked by heavenly peace, joy unspeakable, and warm love from the everlasting spring of God's Triune essence? Then rest in the complete work of Jesus Christ for your salvation. He who justifies you also sanctifies you. "I am sure of this, that He who began a good work in you will bring

---

[62] Edward Mote, "My Hope Is Built On Nothing Less," (1837).

it to completion at the day of Jesus Christ."
(Philippians 1:6) Practice living in Christ's all-sufficient righteous merits.

Doxology

Leaving riches without number,
Born within a cattle stall;
This the everlasting wonder,
Christ was born the Lord of all!
By Thine own eternal Spirit
Rule in all our hearts alone;
By Thine all-sufficient merit,
Raise us to Thy glorious throne.[63]

Pray

O Lord, you left riches without number and emptied yourself to save me! May the blessings of your work flow onto me!

You justified and adopted me. You sanctify me and prepare my soul for eternity with you.

Please grow my assurance of Your love.
You look at me and only see Christ's righteous merits.

Give me peace of conscience.
Increase my joy in the Holy Spirit.

---

[63] *Come, Thou Long Expected Jesus*, Charles Wesley, 1744.

Multiply your graces in my life.

Help me live each day resting on Christ's merits alone. Preserve me in your righteousness alone until my very end.

For Christ's sake, I pray.
Amen.[64]

---

[64] See Benjamin Keach's Catechism (1666), Q. 40. See also Rom. 5:1-5; 14:17; Prov. 4:18; 1 Peter 1:5; 1 John 5:13.

Chapter 8: The Poor Beggar's Hand

The preceding chapters have established what justification is and what it means for Christian living. Yet, how is a person justified? How does Christ's righteousness become your own? Where does such faith in Christ come from? How can you know if your faith is true? The focus of this chapter is the doctrine of *sola fide*: that justification is received by faith alone. More precisely, we affirm that salvation is by God's grace alone through faith *in Christ* alone. "Lord, to whom else 'shall we go? You have the words of eternal life.'"(John 6:68)

Scripture Text: **Romans 3:28**

Therefore, we conclude that a man is justified by faith without the deeds of the law.

Context

Building up to this conclusion, Paul has established that all stand condemned by sin before God. All are without excuse and hopeless if left in that state of condemnation. Any who breaks God's moral law deserves death because God is just. In grace, however, God put forward His own Son as Savior "to be received by faith." (Romans 3:25)

A sinner is justified by God by faith in Christ. The last phrase of this verse cannot be ignored: "without the deeds of the law." (Romans 3:28) If you try to keep God's moral law to earn God's justification for yourself, then you are rejecting the work of Christ on your behalf. You can only be justified by receiving Christ by faith without relying, even a minuscule amount, on your own deeds.

Doctrine
The sole instrument of justification is faith. Faith is receiving and resting on Christ.[65]

The Doctrine Opened
"Therefore, since we have been justified by faith, we have peace with God through our Lord Jesus Christ. Through him we have also obtained access by faith into this grace in which we stand, and we rejoice in hope of the glory of God." (Romans 5:1-2) What is true faith? "Now faith is the assurance of things hoped for, the conviction of things not seen." (Hebrews 11:1)

True faith is first "a knowledge and conviction that everything God reveals in His word is true."[66] It is more than this also, for even Satan would not deny this much. "You believe that God is one; you do well. Even the demons believe—and shudder!" (James 2:19)

If you have true faith, you will joyfully and humbly testify: I have "a deep-rooted assurance, created in me by the Holy Spirit through the gospel, that, out of sheer grace earned for us by Christ, not

---

[65] Second London Baptist Confession of Faith (1677/89), *Chapter 11: Of Justification.*
[66] An Orthodox Catechism, Q. 21.

only others, but I too, have had my sins forgiven, have been made forever right with God, and have been granted salvation."[67]

You are not justified because of the worthiness of your faith. Faith is not a work you do to merit salvation. This is how the Bible speaks of salvation by faith. It is to "take hold of God's strength" (Isaiah 27:5); "receiving Jesus" (John 1:12); "receiving the gift of righteousness" (Romans 5:17 and Acts 26:18). Faith is the instrument God uses. It is an open hand that deserves death but gets life. With that open hand, you grab and take hold of the righteousness of the Redeemer.

Significance

The enemy hates God and His gospel. "If the world hates you, know that it has hated me before it hated you." (John 15:18) Every line of attack has been attempted, including this: turning a person's faith into a work. According to this distortion of the gospel, God saves not by grace alone but by a person's choice to have faith. This false teaching says that you bring your faith to the table as your contribution. Then, God tops off what you lack with His grace. This distortion implies that God's grace is not needed to cover you entirely, only to make up for the deficit that your imperfect faith could not fill.

God's word is clear, however, that even faith is a gift from God: "For by grace you have been saved through faith. And this is not your own doing; it is the gift of God, not a result of works, so that no one may

---

[67] An Orthodox Catechism, Q. 21.

boast." (Ephesians 2:8–9) It is God who confers upon His elect "faith, which together with all the other saving gifts of the Holy Spirit, He purchased for them by His death."[68]

Imagine with me for a moment that there sits a row of beggars. There is nothing attractive about any of them that would deserve the favor of the king. Any favor a beggar may receive will be only on account of his being so needy. The king walks up to the wall against which these invalids sit and commands them to stretch out their hands toward him. He shows them what He commands. His palms face heaven. He closes his eyes. His smile reflects an other-worldly satisfaction and peace.

One beggar scoffs at the command. "Who does he think he is to give us orders like that? I do whatever I want with my hands. No one tells me what to do." Another takes off his hat and shoes, puts them in his hands, then stands up and extends them to the king. "Here, your Majesty, whatever it is you have in mind, let me add what belongs to me as well. You can take these — it's the finest cap of any other man here, and these shoes are only six months old."

No objective observer would doubt the king's generosity. The king scans the row of beggars. His voice rings out in a tone that is just as firm as it is kind: "My command is simple. Poor beggars, stretch out your open hand toward me. Confess that's what you are by simply obeying my word." Faith as a poor

---

[68] Alliance of Confessing Evangelicals, *Cambridge Declaration* (1996), Sola Fide.

beggar's open hand.[69] King Jesus commands all who are poor of spirit to stretch out their hands of faith to receive His grace.

When He shall come with trumpet sound
Oh may I then in him be found
Dressed In His righteousness alone
Faultless to stand before the throne[70]

As the Second London Confession put it: "Faith thus receiving and resting on Christ, and His righteousness, is the alone instrument of justification."[71] In other words, saving faith is to receive and rest in Christ's righteousness personally and continuously. True faith is not something any fallen man can fabricate. True faith is created in you by the Holy Spirit when you grasp the gospel. You grasp with your poor beggar's hand the grace that King Jesus earned and freely gives to you.

---

[69] Henricus Siccama (1692–1746), *Kort Begrip der Waare Godtgeleertheit,* Chapter XVI (On Justification).
[70] Edward Mote, "My Hope Is Built On Nothing Less," (1837).
[71] Second London Baptist Confession of Faith (1677/89), *Chapter 11: Of Justification.*

Doxology

Jesus, I am resting, resting,
         in the joy of what thou art;

I am finding out the greatness
         of thy loving heart.

Thou hast bid me gaze upon thee,
         as thy beauty fills my soul,

For by thy transforming power,
         Thou hast made me whole.

Jesus, I am resting, resting in the joy of what thou art;
I am finding out the greatness of thy loving heart.[72]

Pray

O Lord, thank you for granting me this great salvation
out of your sheer grace.

Please plant a deep-rooted assurance in me by the
power of the Holy Spirit.

Cause me to trust by true faith that I have had my sins
forgiven.

Teach me to fully rest in the promise that Christ has

---

[72] Jean Pigott, "Jesus, I Am Resting, Resting," (1876)

made me forever right with God. Grow my faith in Christ alone who earned eternal life for me.[73]

For Christ's sake, I pray.
Amen.

---

[73] See Hercules Collins, *An Orthodox Catechism,* Question 21.

Chapter 9: The Evidence of Justification

What Is the Fruit Of Union To Christ?

The chapters building up to this point have sought to make this clear: that justification is by God's grace alone, through faith in Christ alone. "[A]s far as the east is from the west, so far does he remove our transgressions from us." (Psalm 103:12) It is God alone who saves you from start to finish. "God purges those He calls to Christ from all sin, both original and actual, whether committed before or after believing; and having faithfully preserved them even to the end, should at last bring them free from every spot and blemish to the enjoyment of glory in His own presence forever."[74]

So then, can a person have real assurance of being united to Christ the Savior? Can you know that you are united to Christ? Is faith merely a feeling? To answer this question, Our Lord Jesus Christ gave a vivid word picture from ancient Israel.

Scripture Text: John 15:3-5

3 Already you are clean because of the word that I have spoken to you. 4 Abide in me, and I in you. As the branch cannot bear fruit by itself, unless it abides in the vine, neither can you, unless you abide in me. 5 I am the vine; you are the branches. Whoever abides

---

[74] Alliance of Confessing Evangelicals, *Cambridge Declaration* (1996), Sola Fide.

in me and I in him, he it is that bears much fruit, for apart from me you can do nothing.

Context

It is dusk on Thursday, less than 24 hours before Jesus of Nazareth will finish His work to purchase His Bride with His own blood. He calls His disciples to rise up. He tells them that the Ruler of this world is coming. He commands His soldiers: "Up and at 'em.'" We will meet the enemy. As they march toward the garden at the foot of the Mt. of Olives, their feet are covered in dust again. He stops and preaches: If you love me you will bear fruit.

To these God-fearing Jewish men, law-keeping meant fulfilling a covenant of works for your salvation. Jesus preaches His gospel to the disciples to correct this man-centered thinking: He assures them, "You are already clean by my word." Likely less than two hours prior, Jesus Christ had washed the dirt off of His disciples' feet onto His body. He told them, I must wash you or else you have no share with me. (John 13:8) Now He tells them, you who are already clean, whom I have justified by my service to you, you will bear my fruit.

Doctrine

True saving faith is never found alone in the person justified — it is always accompanied by other saving graces worked by Christ's love within the believer.[75]

---

[75] Second London Baptist Confession of Faith (1677/89), *Chapter 11: Of Justification.*

The Doctrine Opened

As John Calvin wrote: "It is therefore faith alone which justifies, and yet the faith which justifies is not alone."[76] In His parable about the Sower and the different types of soil, Our Lord Jesus Christ gives three tests of true faith.[77] He declares that false assurance is the stony ground, but true faith is the good ground or heart. This helps us situate the strong warning of James 2:17 "Faith, if it hath not works, is dead, being alone." False assurance does not bear the fruit of the Spirit. False assurance has no root, but true faith has a firm root.

Those who know the risen Christ are transformed. Their message carries on the mature, Christ-exalting tone of the biblical writers that declares: "I count all things [but] loss for the excellency of the knowledge of Christ Jesus my Lord: for whom I have suffered the loss of all things, and do count them [but] dung, that I may win Christ, And be found in him, not having mine own righteousness, which is of the law, but that which is through the faith of Christ, the righteousness which is of God by faith." (Philippians 3:8-9) True faith brings forth fruit with constancy and steadfastness. You can test whether you have true faith in your life. Yet, your life is no grounds for your justification.

---

[76] John Calvin, *Antidote to the Council of Trent,* (1547).
[77] Matthew 13:20 and Luke 8:13 as well as in other places.

Significance

Ponder these questions: Did God stand, so to speak, in eternity past and look down the corridors of time and foresee you choosing to have faith in Him and then doing your best to be a decent person? Is that the basis of your election? Was your salvation predestined upon the condition of you one day bearing the good works for faith and obedience? By no means.

The Bible teaches simply and indisputably that no amount of man-generated good works can ever be sufficient for God to count as worthy of the reward of eternal life.[78] "Who hath saved us, and called us with a holy calling, not according to our works, but according to His own purpose and grace, which was given us in Christ Jesus before the world began." (2 Timothy 1:9) You are saved not because of your future works but only due to God's good and Christ's earned merits for you.

Now, this coin has two sides. Because your salvation is not conditional upon your production of fruit, but by God's work in you, this command becomes a promise. "Whoever abides in me and I in him, he it is that bears much fruit, for apart from me you can do nothing." (John 15:5) You can know that you are united to Christ if He is producing His fruit in your life. You can know that your faith is alive in Christ by the good works He carries out through you who are truly a member of His body. If you are truly His hands and feet, your life will live out His purposes for you.

James 2:26 gives us a striking illustration of

---

[78] The Cannons of Dort, *First Head of Doctrine, Rejection 3.*

this truth. There lies a man. You say, "Hello, sir." He rudely ignores you. You extend your hand to introduce yourself and he snubs you by leaving his own right hand unflinchingly at his side. He doesn't even crack a grin in response to the warmest smile you could muster for a stranger.

Later on, you reflect on that awkward interaction: "That gentleman is one of the coldest prudes I've ever met." Yet there is a good reason for this. You were trying to greet a corpse. That lifeless man's soul had already left his body. He was lifeless because he was dead. "For as the body apart from the spirit is dead, so also faith apart from works is dead." If you are cold, loveless, and lifeless toward the Bride of Christ, then it is possible that you only have a dead faith. There can be no objective evidence of salvation without an increasing transformation of life.

In the Upper Room, Jesus had torn the bread. He has poured out the fruit of the vine. His disciples had eaten His body and drunk His blood. Those sacramental elements became one with their bodies through digestion. Now Jesus teaches them: "Abide in your union to Me through faith. As you abide in me, my love, my righteousness, and my obedience will work their way into our lives. My righteous fruit will grow in your lives." Any holy fruit your life bears was sourced by the Son, watered by His word, matured by His Spirit, and increased by the pruning of the Father. Christ Himself promises to provide evidence in your life of true justification.

Doxology

*Pardon for sin and a peace that endureth
Thy own dear presence to cheer and to guide.*

*Strength for today and bright hope for tomorrow,
Blessings all mine, with ten thousand beside.*

*Great is thy faithfulness... Great is thy faithfulness...
Great is thy faithfulness, Lord unto me!* [79]

Pray

*O Lord, thank you that through my union to Christ,
you declare me to be already clean. Train me to abide
in Christ. Thank you that, by Your Spirit, Christ
abides in me.I confess: just as a branch cannot bear
fruit by itself unless it abides in the vine, neither can I
unless you abide in Christ. You promise: "Whoever
abides in me and I in him, he it is that bears much
fruit." I trust You.* [80]

*For Christ's sake, I pray.
Amen.*

---

[79] William Runyan, "Great Is Thy Faithfulness," (1923).
[80] See John 15:1–17.

Chapter 10: For Christ's Sake Alone

Beware of Hollow Peddlers

There is a flavor of religion — there always has been, in fact — that focuses your mind on how you are feeling. When this version of religion is preached it takes the tone of a teenager who thinks they can talk you into dating their friend again, the one you broke up with last summer, during one of your mood swings.

Such imposters urge you to connect with "Jesus." In reality, those deceivers are trying to get people to connect emotionally with an idol fabricated in their minds. They plagiarize Our Savior's glorious name. These false teachers are hollow peddlers.[81] Be warned: to such Christ will declare, "Away from me. I never knew you." (Matthew 7:23) These are not ministers of Our Lord Jesus Christ. They don't serve Christ. They serve man's pride and undermine the name of the only true God.

You are not saved because you chose to love Jesus. The reality is not that God couldn't find anywhere else to live until you found room in your heart for him. You would have no love for God at all unless God first loved you. (1 John 4:19) Your salvation is accomplished by the mediatorial work of the historical Christ alone. His sinless life and substitutionary atonement alone are sufficient for our

---

[81] 2 Corinthians 2:17

justification and reconciliation with the Father.[82] The only thing we contribute to our salvation is our sin. It is only for Christ's sake that we are saved.

Scripture Text: Ephesians 2:8–10

For by grace are ye saved through faith; and that not of yourselves: [it is] the gift of God: Not of works, lest any man should boast. For we are His workmanship, created in Christ Jesus unto good works, which God hath before ordained that we should walk in them.

Context

The Bible exalts Christ not only as the founder of our faith but also as the One for whose sake we are saved. Scripture uses language that depicts an instantaneous change of status. You were a neglected orphan under the abusive tyranny of Satan, but now you are adopted in Christ. You were naked, humiliated, and exposed to deadly elements in this present evil age (Galatians 1:4), but now you are clothed in Christ's righteousness. "I will greatly rejoice in the LORD; my soul shall exult in my God, for He has clothed me with the garments of salvation; He has covered me with the robe of righteousness." (Isaiah 61:10)

Justification is an instantaneous declaration. Because of Christ's finished work on behalf of His people, "we have also obtained access by faith into this grace in which we stand." (Romans 5:2) This declaration of right standing in Christ is not to be confused with the fruit of union with Christ.

---

[82] Alliance of Confessing Evangelicals, *Cambridge Declaration* (1996), Thesis Two: Solus Christus.

Justification is the root. God Himself examines those who pretend to be His Son's wedding guests. "[H]e saw there a man who had no wedding garment." and cast Him out. (Matthew 22:11) Your union to Christ through faith clothes you in His righteousness. Union to Christ adopts believers as children of God. Christ's Sonship to the Father binds believers to God as "fellow heirs with Christ." (Romans 8:17)

Grateful living is the fruit. Just "as you received Christ Jesus the Lord, so walk in him, rooted and built up in him and established in the faith." (Colossians 2:6-7) The fruit does not save you. Christ's righteousness alone clothes you for the wedding supper of the Lamb.

Doctrine

God justifies for Christ's sake alone, not for anything in man.[83]

The Doctrine Opened

Once again, it is crucial that each doctrine in the order of salvation be handled precisely, without taking from truths that fall under another. For instance, justification is an instant declaration, but sanctification is a gradual process. "For by a single offering He has perfected for all time those who are being sanctified." (Hebrews 10:14) If we teach that a person must gradually become more righteous to be justified, we misunderstand God's grace. On the other

---

[83] Second London Baptist Confession of Faith (1677/89), *Chapter 11: Of Justification.*

hand, if we teach a person will not increasingly grow in sanctification after being justified, we misunderstand the law of Christ.[84]

God does not leave you unconverted to then apply His righteousness slowly over time into you. You are never partially justified. "For by a single offering He has perfected for all time those who are being sanctified." (Romans 6:17) God does not count you righteous for showing a certain type of emotion (though the regenerate will feel deep contrition). Even after being saved, no amount of future obedience could ever pay off the eternal debt you owe him. "[A]ll our righteous deeds are like a polluted garment." (Isaiah 64:6) You are justified for the sake of Christ alone. Rather, He sees you in your sin, gives you a new heart, unites you to Christ, and clothes you with all of Christ's merits at once. Then God looks at you and sees you fully clothed in Christ and, in that same moment, God declares you righteous.

Significance

Reflect on this doctrine in light of a simple illustration. A rising warrior within his nation's army promised his best friend that He would always protect his family. When that warrior became king, the only surviving relative was one of his sons, the one paralyzed at a young age and, now a lame man. When the fierce king summoned the paralytic, He would have been terrified. Yet, the king invited him to share every meal next to him at the royal table. He was family. The lame man threw himself at the king's feet.[85]

---

[84] Galatians 6:2: "fulfill the law of Christ."

Since the favor he enjoyed was nothing he merited or contributed to in the slightest, it was a favor he could always trust and never fear losing. No man in the entire kingdom could strip him of it. In the same way, since your justification is for Christ's sake alone, you can have assurance of salvation. No one can strip you of God's favor to you since it is all for Christ:

> *Who shall lay anything to the charge of God's elect? It is God that justifieth. Who is he that condemneth? It is Christ that died, yea rather, that is risen again, who is even at the right hand of God, who also maketh intercession for us. Who shall separate us from the love of Christ? (Romans 8:34–35, KJV).*

The paralytic would have understood very well how the blessings he enjoyed were of no merit of his own. It was not because of his speed. He couldn't even walk. It was not for his military conquests; he couldn't even ride a horse. It wasn't for his strength or bravery. He had to sit around the house all day. It wasn't even for his faith or grateful loyalty to the king. He received the king's mercy and generosity purely for his father's sake. God saved you for Christ's sake alone.

---

[85] 2 Samuel 9:6.

Doxology

Because the sinless Savior died,
My sinful soul is counted free

For God the Just is satisfied
To look on Him and pardon me[86]

Pray from Matthew 6:9 and An Orthodox Catechism – Question 142

Our Father in heaven, hallowed be your name! [87]

Help me to know you, bless, worship, and praise you
for all your works and all that shines forth from them:

Your almighty power, wisdom, kindness, justice,
mercy, and truth.

Help me to direct all my living – what I think, say, and
do.

May I never blaspheme your name.

May my life always bring you honor and praised. [88]

For Christ's sake, I pray.

---

[86] Charitie Lees Bancroft, "Before The Throne Of God Above," (1863).

[87] "Pray then like this: 'Our Father in heaven, hallowed be your name.'" Matthew 6:9.

[88] Hercules Collins, *An Orthodox Catechism,* Question 142, (1680).

Amen.

Chapter 11: The Timing of Justification

Were You Justified in Eternity Past?

Satan's obsession is to fight against God's glory. There is no clearer way to do so than to undermine God's word about salvation. One way in which Satan has done this is by confusing God's sovereignty in salvation with fatalism. Some have called this distorted notion "hyper-Calvinism," though the exiled French pastor, John Calvin, would have wanted nothing to do with it. Calvin, whom Christ used to reform His church in Geneva, Switzerland, was committed to giving God's people God's word clearly and directly. He would have opposed fatalism for it is a false teaching that all true biblical (and Calvinistic) preachers have passionately refuted in every generation.

     The Bible does teach that God decreed from all eternity to justify His elect. (Gal. 3:8, 1 Pet. 1:2, 1 Tim. 2:6). Yet, does that mean that God justified you before the foundation of the world? If you are elect of God unto salvation, does that mean you were justified in your mother's womb? Fatalism teaches that man has no responsibility since God saves according to His eternal decree. If God justified you in eternity past then your life is of no real consequence. You would be like a preprogramed robot; your covenant relationship with God would be artificial. Is that what the Bible teaches about the timing of your justification?

Scripture Text: **Titus 3:4-7**

4 But when the goodness and loving kindness of God our Savior appeared, 5 He saved us, not because of works done by us in righteousness, but according to His own mercy, by the washing of regeneration and renewal of the Holy Spirit, 6 whom He poured out on us richly through Jesus Christ our Savior, 7 so that being justified by His grace we might become heirs according to the hope of eternal life.

Context

Remember in Chapter 1 we sought to establish the reality from scripture that you and I were born spiritually dead. Numerous places in scripture teach that Adam's race is spiritually incapable of repenting and believing. One such place is Colossians 1:21-22 21: "[Y]ou, who once were alienated and hostile in mind, doing evil deeds, He has now reconciled in His body of flesh by His death, in order to present you holy and blameless and above reproach before him." The same souls that God justified were once hostile toward Him. Those souls previously alienated from God, Christ now presents blameless. This He can do because Christ reconciled them by His death.

> *How deep the Father's love for us, how vast beyond all measure;*
>
> *That He should give His only son, to make a wretch His treasure.* [89]

The Bible does teach that in the fullness of time, Christ died for the sins of His people and rose

---

[89] Stuart Townend, "How Deep The Father's Love For Us," (1996).

again for their justification. (Rom. 4:25) So, when is a Christian justified? Were you justified the moment Christ rose from the dead? What takes place in time and space to effectuate this? According to Titus 3, Christ appeared on earth to effectuate your salvation with His life, death, resurrection, and ascension. Yet, how does God make a wretch His treasure? The salvation Christ accomplished for you does not become yours until the Holy Spirit applies it personally to your soul.

Doctrine

You are justified in one distinct and irreversible moment: when the Holy Spirit applies Christ to you personally.[90]

The Doctrine Opened

The Puritan Thomas Goodwin (1600–1680), saw three "moments" of justification. First, in eternity past, in the covenant of redemption, the substitutionary double imputation took place: The Father, Son, and Spirit decreed to make the righteousness of the Son a gift to His Bride and that His cursed death would purchase their pardon. This gospel is the "wisdom of God, which God decreed before the ages for our glory." (1 Corinthians 2:7) Second, the redemption of God's elect people was transacted in history once and for all by the finished work of Christ on the cross. As federal head and covenantal Mediator Christ accomplished God's

---

[90] Second London Baptist Confession of Faith (1677/89), *Chapter 11: Of Justification.*

decreed mission. "I glorified you on earth, having accomplished the work that you gave me to do." (John 17:4) Third, when an individual personally lays hold of the forgiveness of sins and Christ's righteousness through the effectual calling and regeneration of the Holy Spirit. "God's love has been poured into our hearts through the Holy Spirit who has been given to us." (Romans 5:5)

The whole scope of God's decree to justify you is breathtaking. Understanding this theology, however, does not justify you. You are not justified until the Holy Spirit washes you with regeneration. "[H]e saved us, not because of works done by us in righteousness, but according to His own mercy, by the washing of regeneration and renewal of the Holy Spirit." (Titus 3:5) This is what your baptism illustrates. You remain dead in Adam's curse until the Spirit renews you or makes you new in Christ, joined to Him who is the last Adam, the firstborn of the new creation. "Therefore, if anyone is in Christ, He is a new creation." (2 Corinthians 5:17)

In justification, Christ's righteousness is imputed to us as the only possible satisfaction of God's perfect justice. How does this happen? Paul wrote that your regeneration takes place through Christ pouring out the Holy Spirit richly upon His church, "so that being justified by His grace we might become heirs according to the hope of eternal life." (Titus 3:7) Only those are saved who by true faith are grafted into Christ. Only after the Holy Spirit unites you to Christ can you enjoy all of His blessings.

Significance

The washing of the Spirit is a spiritual reality. To grow our faith, He instituted a sacrament to make this gospel word visible. Baptism is the dramatization of the Holy Spirit's washing of regeneration. Baptism is a celebration of your justification. The elect have a legal right to justification but do not yet possess it before regeneration. The elect can only possess it once they profess faith in Christ. "In him you also, when you heard the word of truth, the gospel of your salvation, and believed in him, were sealed with the promised Holy Spirit." (Ephesians 1:13) The salvation that Christ accomplished is only truly yours if you have received the Holy Spirit's washing of regeneration. Only then are you united to your Savior, Jesus Christ. Only then is your sin washed away by His blood. Only then can you claim His righteousness as your own.

Doxology

Mild He lays His glory by,
born that man no more may die

Born to raise the sons of earth,
born to give them second birth

Hark the herald angels sing,
"Glory to the newborn King" [91]

---

[91] Charles Wesley, Hark, The Harold Angels Sing! (1739)

Pray through Matthew 6:10 and Romans 8:30

Hallowed by Thy name, O Triune Creator, my God.

Thank you for electing me to belong to you, O God my Father. Thank you for calling me to belong to you by the word of God.

Thank you for regenerating me and washing me, O Holy Spirit. Thank you for accomplishing my justification, O God the Son.

Thank you for sanctifying me, O Holy Spirit. I trust that one day you will glorify me in Christ.

May your kingdom come. May your will be done on earth as it is in heaven. [92]

For Christ's sake, I pray.
Amen.

---

[92] See Matthew 6:10 and Romans 8:30.

Chapter 12: When A Justified Person Sins

Can you lose your salvation? Can a true believer reject Christ and shipwreck their faith? Once you are justified, can that status before God ever be reversed? It does stand to reason that if your salvation hinges upon you choosing God, then by that same power you can un-choose Him. However, this contradicts all that the Bible teaches about our justification. Such a notion also stands against the direct words of the Good Shepherd.

Scripture Text: **John 10:27-29**

27 My sheep hear my voice, and I know them, and they follow me. 28 I give them eternal life, and they will never perish, and no one will snatch them out of my hand. 29 My Father, who has given them to me, is greater than all, and no one is able to snatch them out of the Father's hand.

Context

In this glorious chapter, our Lord Jesus Christ explains His mission to save you in this clear and rich metaphor. He is the Good Shepherd. He calls His sheep by name. His sheep (not all sheep, but only and all of the sheep that are His) follow their Good Shepherd. Those sheep that belong to Him are safe. He and His Father hold them. He lays down His life for His sheep. No one can snatch them out of His hand. They will never perish.

Christ could not have expressed the security of His sheep in any stronger terms than He did in these verses. In this glorious process, He gives at least nine reasons why His sheep will never perish. If you hear Christ's voice, you do not need to fear losing Him. The word of God promises: 1) Christ knows you; 2) you will follow Him; 3) He gives you eternal life; 4) you are in Christ's hand; no one can snatch you out of Christ's hand; 5) you were given to Christ by the Father; 6) the Father's decree for your salvation is greater than all; 7) you are in the Father's hand; 8) Christ gives you His word that you will never perish from this life you have in Him because 9) He laid down His life for you, His sheep.

Doctrine
If justified, always justified. God continues to forgive the sins of those who are justified.[93]

The Doctrine Opened
If God has justified you, you will not repent of Christ and return to the bondage of sin. You will not do this because God's word says that if you are born of God you cannot sin in such a way. "Whosoever is born of God doth not commit sin; for His seed remains in him: and He cannot sin, because He is born of God" (1 John 3:9, KJV) This verse can sound like once you are born of God (regenerated) then you can't sin. Yet,

---

[93] Second London Baptist Confession of Faith (1677/89), *Chapter 11: Of Justification.*

this is John's way of preaching. He preaches using stark, binary opposites. Light or darkness. Life or death. Peace or trouble. In 1 John 3:9, he wrote that a true Christian cannot sin. 1 John 1:8, he wrote: "If we say we have no sin, we deceive ourselves, and the truth is not in us."

So, what does the Bible teach? Does the corruption of your sinful nature that you inherited from Adam remain in you after you are regenerated? The last paragraph on the doctrine of sin in the Second London Confession of Faith answers with an unconfused "Yes." The good news is that once Christ justifies you, the Holy Spirit leads you in mortifying (or killing) your remaining sin. "And do not grieve the Holy Spirit of God, by whom you were sealed for the day of redemption." (Ephesians 4:30) The mortification of sin is worked out in you by the same faith in Christ that led you to be justified by His grace alone.

While you have remaining sin in your flesh (Romans 7:17-20),[94] if God has justified you, you will never be declared guilty again. God's decree to elect you is unchangeable. He will never withdraw His Holy Spirit from you. Even when you fall into a tempting pit, God will not let you fall out of His hands. He protects you from forfeiting your state of justification. The Holy Spirit in you guards you from your fleshly temptations to blaspheme your Savior. Once justified, you cannot perish into everlasting

---

[94] 17 So now it is no longer I who do it, but sin that dwells within me. 18 For I know that nothing good dwells in me, that is, in my flesh. For I have the desire to do what is right, but not the ability to carry it out. 19 For I do not do the good I want, but the evil I do not want is what I keep on doing. 20 Now if I do what I do not want, it is no longer I who do it, but sin that dwells within me.

destruction. You can't disfellowship with God because God is the One who chose you. While you were His enemy, He sent His Son to lay down His life for you. "For if while we were enemies we were reconciled to God by the death of His Son, much more, now that we are reconciled, shall we be saved by His life." (Romans 5:10)

Significance

The congregation had gathered at a park for an outdoor worship service one warm Sunday. A little boy walked up to a pastor after the service and asked: "What happens if I get baptized, but then after that, I still sin?" The pastor explained to the young believer that his justification is legal. A judge either finds you innocent or guilty. If you are found innocent, you enjoy all the rights and privileges of an innocent person. You were bound in the chains of sin. Jesus has all authority. He is the great Judge appointed by His Father. Jesus saved you. Satan accuses you, but no one can change the Judge's verdict. Remember the words of your Savior: "If the Son sets you free, you will be free indeed." (John 8:36)

This sincere nine-year-old echoes what Christians have wrestled with in every generation. Most famously, a professor in a Dutch seminary who deviated from Calvin's teaching a couple hundred years prior taught a doctrine that is now the most popularly held view. This professor's name was Jacobus Arminius. He taught that a true believer could fall from justifying faith — losing God's grace and salvation altogether.

If Arminius was right, your sin makes God's grace subservient, not sovereign. It would mean that your sin rules over you more than Christ's righteousness. It would make the remaining sin in your flesh more powerful than the new life that Christ breathed into your soul by His Spirit when God regenerated your internal person. It would make Adam's curse more binding than Christ's blessing. It would make Satan outside of you more dominant than the Holy Spirit within you. It would mean that your Accuser is more just than your Advocate.

The Bible teaches that God's grace is not subservient to your sin. God's grace is sovereign. "Salvation belongs to the LORD!" (Jonah 2:9) The Bible teaches that your sin does not rule over you more than Christ's righteousness. "For sin will have no dominion over you, since you are not under law but under grace." (Romans 6:14)

The Bible teaches that the remaining sin in your flesh is not more powerful than the new life that Christ breathed into your soul by His Spirit when God regenerated you. That Christ "may grant you to be strengthened with power through His Spirit in your inner being." (Ephesians 3:16) The Bible teaches that Christ's victory cancelled Adam's curse for those God justified. "He disarmed the rulers and authorities and put them to open shame, by triumphing over them." (Colossians 2:15)

The Bible teaches that Holy Spirit within you breaks Satan's dominion over you. "[L]et the peace of Christ rule in your hearts" (Colossians 3:18) The Bible teaches that your Advocate silences your Accuser. Jesus cleanses your life, His dwelling temple and "established strength because of your foes, to still the enemy and the avenger." (Psalm 8:2, Matthew 21:16)

Because Arminius' teaching is impossible in the light of Scripture, there must be a different explanation for why some apostatize. Why do some claim to be true believers for a season only to abandon the faith later on? Why do some claim to "un-convert" from Christianity? Why do some who once thought they were justified now reject Christ and His word? John answers this question directly: "[T]hey were not of us; for if they had been of us, they would have continued with us. But they went out, that it might become plain that they all are not of us." (1 John 2:19)

Though you are regenerated, you have remaining sin in your flesh. Yes, you will battle against sin after you are justified until you breathe your final breath. "If we say we have no sin, we deceive ourselves, and the truth is not in us." (1 John 1:8) Remember, Christ has overcome all temptation already. Christ "in every respect has been tempted as we are, yet without sin." (Hebrews 4:15) Rest in His power, not your own. Christ's "Spirit helps us in our weakness." (Romans 8:26) Know that no weapon or accusation "that is fashioned against you shall succeed," (Isaiah 54:17) because it was God who justified you in Christ. His power is at work within you. Christ "is able to do far more abundantly than all that we ask or think, according to the power at work within us." (Ephesians 3:20)

One of the founders of the Reformed Church in Germany in the late 1500s, Caspar Olevianus, grasped this comforting spiritual reality. He remarked:

we have "much more righteousness in Christ than sin in [ourselves]. Indeed, a Christian has more righteousness than do all the angels in heaven."[95] No matter how great your sin, greater still is Christ's righteousness for you. "My grace is sufficient for you, for my power is made perfect in weakness." (2 Corinthians 12:9)

Doxology

When Satan tempts me to despair
And tells me of the guilt within,
Upward I look and see Him there
Who made an end to all my sin. [96]

Pray

O Lord, Help me to trust your promise:
That You do see my sins and you grieve at them so
For when I am sinning your love I don't know.
Yet, even when I am sinning, Your grace does abound,
Ensuring my justified status is sound.
No wrath is awakened in You at my sin
Because Christ appeased it — to say so again.[97]

For Christ's Sake, I pray.
Amen.

---

[95] Olevianus, Caspar. "A firm foundation: An aid to interpreting the Heidelberg Catechism, transl. LD Bierma." *Grand Rapids: Baker Books* 90, no. 8 (1995). 119.

[96] Charitie Lees Bancroft, "Before The Throne Of God Above," (1863).

[97] Adapted from Milton Vincent, *A Gospel Primer: For Christians*, p. 75.

Chapter 13: Justification In All of Scripture

Only Diamond Cuts Diamond

When you read your Bible, you rely on God's Holy Spirit to help you understand His word as He intends. You pray that the same Spirit who breathed out the scriptures will assist you in interpreting His word correctly. As you and I learn to practice correct biblical interpretation, we employ the tools God's word gives to do so. This is called hermeneutics, or principles of interpretation. One important hermeneutical tool is called New Testament priority.

This ancient tool has assisted God's people over the centuries. Augustine, for instance, wrote: "The New is in the Old concealed; the Old is in the New revealed." [98] Similarly, an early confessional Particular Baptist, Nehemiah Coxe, agreed with the Reformed interpretive principle when he wrote, "...the best interpreter of the Old Testament is the Holy Spirit speaking to us in the new." [99] A phrase common among the Puritans to express this principle was: "Only diamond cuts diamond."

Now, a real challenge for all students of God's word is to consistently applying this principle of New Testament priority. All of scripture has one divine

---

[98] Fitzgerald, Allan, and John C. Cavadini, eds. *Augustine through the ages: An encyclopedia.* Eerdmans Publishing, 1999. Grand Rapids, MI: Eerdmans Publishing, (1999), p. 144.
[99] Nehemiah Coxe and John Owen, *Covenant Theology from Adam to Christ,* ed. Ronald D. Miller, James M. Renihan, and Fransisco Orozco (Palmdale, CA: Reformed Baptist Academic Press, 2005), 36.

Author. When God illuminates His word to His people, the glorious jewels of His gospel sparkle from even the most shadowy portions of the Bible. This is certainly the case with justification.

So, whom did God save before Christ finished His work? How were Old Testament believers saved? How can we accurately express the mysterious truths contained in all of God's word?

Scripture Text: **Romans 4:20-25**

20 No unbelief made him waver concerning the promise of God, but he grew strong in his faith as he gave glory to God, 21 fully convinced that God was able to do what He had promised. 22 That is why his faith was "counted to him as righteousness." 23 But the words "it was counted to him" were not written for his sake alone, 24 but for ours also. It will be counted to us who believe in him who raised from the dead Jesus our Lord, 25 who was delivered up for our trespasses and raised for our justification.

Context

The New Testament makes it clear that God counted believers in the Old Testament as righteous. In Romans chapter 4, Paul provides a Spirit-inspired interpretation of God's promise to Abraham. What's more, this passage states that God's purpose in justifying Abraham through imputation was for the sake of the church. Abraham's life and the record thereof in scripture is a gift to strengthen your grasp of how God justifies sinners by faith in God's promise alone. God grew Abraham's faith that God was able to do what He had promised. Abraham learned to trust in God's sovereign saving power, not his own. The result: Abraham gave glory to God.

What promise from God did Abraham believe? We read of God's promise to Abraham in Genesis 12–17. Specifically, in Genesis 17:7, God says: "I will establish my covenant between me and you and your offspring after you throughout their generations for an everlasting covenant, to be God to you and to your offspring after you." The principle of New Testament priority controls our understanding of this promise.[100] We must ask, "What does the New Testament tell us about God's promise to Abraham?" The answer to this question is significant. God counted Abraham's faith in this promise to him as righteousness. Galatians 3:16 says, "Now the promises were made to Abraham and his offspring. It does not say, 'And to offsprings,' referring to many, but referring to one, 'And to your offspring,' who is Christ."

Doctrine

God has always justified His people in the same way, even before Christ's incarnation and work. That is, by grace alone through faith in Christ alone.[101]

---

[100] Tom Hicks has pointed out the erroneous conclusions that we can make if we neglect to let the Bible interpret the Bible, using the principle of New Testament priority: "Dispensationalists think Genesis 17:7 establishes an everlasting promise to national Israel, and they read their interpretation into the New Testament, convinced that God has future plans for national Israel. Paedobaptists, on the other hand, think the promise in Genesis 17:7 is the covenant of grace with Abraham and all his physical children, which leads to the baptism of infants in the New Testament and to churches intentionally mixed with believers and unbelievers." Retrieved October 24, 2023 from: https://founders.org/articles/hermeneutics-new-testament-priority

The Doctrine Opened

When you read your Bible, you can see the gospel of Jesus Christ on every page. The Old Testament foreshadows His work. The New Testament confirms and applies it to your life. Scripture in its entirety reassures you of God's faithfulness to His promise to justify freely all those for whom Christ died.

This glorious promise was first given not to Abraham but as a curse on the serpent following Adam's banishment from the Garden of Eden. God promised: I will put enmity between you and the woman, and between your offspring and her offspring; He shall bruise your head, and you shall bruise His heel." From Adam and Even onward, all who believed that God would fulfill His promise were putting their faith in Christ's future work. Notice the same doctrines of justification in this pregnant verse:

1. God promises to regenerate. God would work a change in the hearts of His elect. Those born under Adam's curse are born loving sin, under Satan's rule. Yet God promises: "I will put enmity" between them and Satan.

2. God promises redemption. The Seed of Eve will execute God's victory: "He shall bruise your head." God's sovereign decree will come to pass at God's appointed time.

3. God promises that sin will be punished. The promised seed will suffer the just wrath of

---

[101] Second London Baptist Confession of Faith (1677/89), *Chapter 11: Of Justification.*

God against sin from the Serpent's fangs: "You shall bruise His heal."

4. God promises life. Adam named his wife Eve, which means life. Through her will come one who will bring new life. God's Promised Seed will suffer, but the Serpent will not crush His head. He lives!

In the 1600s, Francis Turretin was a theologian based in Geneva who followed John Calvin's tradition. He offered helpful insights into the meaning of Revelation 13:8, which reveals God's book of life that contains names "written before the foundation of the world in the book of life of the Lamb who was slain." Turretin understood from this passage that God laid upon Christ the sins of all of the elect who ever lived, from every generation before and after Christ. Yet, Turretin taught that God did not immediately require payment for them. God imputed the debt to Christ, but He did not execute payment until His earthly ministry. God the Father designated God the Son as the Lamb slain before the foundation of the world. (Revelation 13:8)

This accounts for how God could justly cover Abraham with Christ's righteousness by faith in God's promise alone. Abraham had faith in God's ability to fully carry out His salvation through the seed God promised Him. Abraham put his faith in the future work of Christ. God could justly count as a satisfactory payment for all of Abraham's sins the future penal substitutionary death that Christ would execute on the cross.

Further revelation prepared the way for Christ's work. At the top of Mount Sinai, God opened Moses' eyes to behold Christ's glorious work in heaven. The ceremonial law was a gracious gift to God's elect. It was an earthly shadow of a heavenly reality. Hebrews 8:5 reveals that those under the ceremonial laws of Moses "serve a copy and shadow of the heavenly things. For when Moses was about to erect the tent, he was instructed by God, saying, 'See that you make everything according to the pattern that was shown you on the mountain.'"

Yet, it was only that, an earthly pointer to a spiritual reality. Hebrews 10:4 explains that "it is impossible for the blood of bulls and goats to take away sins." Hebrews 9:9 confirms that "gifts and sacrifices were offered that cannot perfect the conscience of the worshiper." The Lord showed Moses a pattern, a sacrament.

God made the work of Christ visible in the sacrificial system. God's old covenant people experienced justifying salvation. They trusted in God's promise to forgive their sins by grace alone through faith. God forgave not because the blood of bulls and goats was sufficient payment, but because of their faith in what was conveyed to them in Christ in the promises and sacrifices that God would steadfastly show them covenantal grace.

Significance

God applied the glorious gospel of justification by faith in God's promised seed, who is Christ with power. In this way, God justified Abel, Seth, Enoch,

Noah, Abraham, Isaac, Jacob, Moses, David, and the believing Israelites. Regardless of how much or little of God's word sinners had at any given point in history, all of God's elect throughout every century who received by faith God's promised gracious Savior experienced complete justification. All those who heard God's word, repented, believed, and trusted in God's gracious salvation — His steadfast love which binds God to fulfill His promise — God was faithful and just to save.

You can find assurance of God's faithfulness to forgive sins and justify those who trust in Christ as the fulfillment of God's promise, along with the great cloud of witnesses. All of scripture confirms God's covenant faithfulness, fulfilled with Christ's atoning work on your behalf. See the doctrine of justification by faith in Christ alone in all of the Bible:

Psalm 32:1 "Blessed is the one whose transgression is forgiven, whose sin is covered."

Psalm 85:2 "You forgave the iniquity of your people; you covered all their sin."

Isaiah 55:7 "Let the wicked forsake his way, and the unrighteous man his thoughts; let him return to the LORD, that He may have compassion on him, and to our God, for He will abundantly pardon."

Psalm 65:3 "When iniquities prevail against me, you atone for our transgressions."

Psalm 130:3 "If you, O LORD, should mark iniquities, O Lord, who could stand?"

Micah 7:18–19 "Who is a God like you, pardoning iniquity and passing over transgression for the remnant of his inheritance? He does not retain His anger forever, because he delights in steadfast love. He will again have compassion on us; He will tread our iniquities underfoot. You will cast all our sins into the depths of the sea."

Worship your faithful Savior as God reveals to you from all of the Bible His gracious, faithful, loving justification of one such as you, for Christ's sake alone. Let all of scripture fill your mind with the glory of God in saving you. Let the Spirit stir your heart with God's loving, redeeming, assuring grace. Take up all of the Bible and read of your God-planned, God-accomplished, and God-applied redemption. God is my Savior! He confirms this over and over again from every page of Scripture. If you are justified, this blessed truth is yours. Know this!

You are the poor beggar in the dirt, but if you are justified, then your hands can now hold, and your heart can hear the very words of your Savior.

You are the orphan born in poverty, but if you are justified, then you were adopted to enjoy all of the Father's mansion.

You are the fugitive at midnight, but if you are justified, you already have your permanent citizenship papers of heaven's kingdom.

You are the lame cripple hideaway, but if you are justified, then you are now healed to run, and play, and climb in the King's private gardens.

You are the starving homeless child, but if you are justified, then you now have a reserved seat for every meal of every day at the victory banquet table next to Jesus Christ Himself.

Out of love for your Savior, search out and marvel at God's glory in every sentence of every chapter of every book in His glorious Bible. Know that they that bear witness about me is what Christ says in John 5:39. As you read all of God's word, discuss all of God's word, and hear all of God's word preached, may the Holy Spirit assure you more, and more, that you are justified truly, fully, and finally...

for Christ's sake alone.

Doxology

I oft read with pleasure, to soothe or engage,
Isaiah's wild measure and John's simple page;

But 'en when they pictured the blood sprinkled
tree Jehovah Tsidkenu seemed nothing to me.

When free grace awoke me by light from on high,
Then legal fears shook me, I trembled to die;

No refuge, no safety in self could I see—
Jehovah Tsidkenu my Saviour must be.

My terrors all vanished before the sweet name;
My guilty fears banished, with boldness I came

To drink at the fountain, life-giving and free
Jehovah Tsidkenu is all things to me.[102]

Pray through Exodus 34:6-7 and Psalm 25:11
O LORD, you are my LORD!

You are a God merciful and gracious, slow to anger,
and abounding in steadfast love and faithfulness,

You keep Your steadfast love for thousands,
forgiving iniquity, transgressions, and sin. [103]

Pardon my guilt, for it is great, O Lord,

For your name's sake!

Thank you for my justification. [104]

For Christ's Sake, I pray.
Amen.

---

[102] Jehovah Tsidkenu by Robert Murray M'Cheyne (1867).
[103] See Exodus 34:6-7.
[104] See Psalm 25:11.

Second London Baptist Confession of Faith (1689)

Chapter 11: Of Justification[105]

1. Those whom God effectually calls, He also freely justifies, 1 not by infusing righteousness into them, but by pardoning their sins, and by accounting and accepting their persons as righteous; 2 not for anything wrought in them, or done by them, but for Christ's sake alone; 3 not by imputing faith itself, the act of believing, or any other evangelical obedience to them, as their righteousness; but by imputing Christ's active obedience unto the whole law, and passive obedience in His death for their whole and sole righteousness by faith, 4 which faith they have not of themselves; it is the gift of God. 5

1. Romans 3:24, 8:30
2. Romans 4:5-8, Ephesians 1:7
3. 1 Corinthians 1:30-31, Romans 5:17–19
4. Philippians 3:8-9; Ephesians 2:8–10
5. John 1:12, Romans 5:17

2. Faith thus receiving and resting on Christ and His righteousness, is the alone instrument of justification; 6 yet is not alone in the person justified, but is ever

---

[105] Second London Baptist Confession of Faith (1677/89), *Chapter 11: Of Justification.*

accompanied with all other saving graces, and is no dead faith, but works by love. 7

6. Romans 3:28

7. Galatians 5:6, James 2:17, 22, 26

3. Christ, by His obedience and death, did fully discharge the debt of all those who are justified; and did, by the sacrifice of himself in the blood of His cross, undergoing in their stead the penalty due to them, make a proper, real, and full satisfaction to God's justice in their behalf; 8 yet, in as much as He was given by the Father for them, and His obedience and satisfaction accepted in their stead, and both freely, not for anything in them, 9 their justification is only of free grace, that both the exact justice and rich grace of God might be glorified in the justification of sinners. 10

8. Hebrews 10:14; 1 Peter 1:18–19; Isaiah 53:5-6

9. Romans 8:32; 2 Corinthians 5:21

10. Romans 3:26; Ephesians 1:6-7, 2:7

4. God did from all eternity decree to justify all the elect, 11 and Christ did in the fullness of time die for their sins, and rise again for their justification; 12 nevertheless, they are not justified personally, until the Holy Spirit in time does actually apply Christ to them. 13

11. Galatians 3:8, 1 Peter 1:2, 1 Timothy 2:6

12. Romans 4:25

13. Colossians 1:21-22, Titus 3:4-7

5. God continues to forgive the sins of those that are justified, 14 and although they can never fall from the state of justification, 15 yet they may, by their sins, fall under God's fatherly displeasure; 16 and in that condition they usually do not have the light of His countenance restored to them, until they humble themselves, beg pardon, and renew their faith and repentance. 17

14. Matthew 6:12, 1 John 1:7, 9

15. John 10:28

16. Psalms 89:31-33

17. Psalms 32:5, Psalms 51, Matthew 26:75

6. The justification of believers under the Old Testament was, in all these respects, one and the same with the justification of believers under the New Testament. 18

18. Galatians 3:9; Romans 4:22-24

ABOUT THE AUTHOR

Jason David Edwards grew up as a missionary kid in Brazil but has called Colorado home since 2011, where he and his beloved wife are raising their four kids.

He was prepared for pastoral ministry by our gracious Lord through Calvary Redeeming Grace Church in Lakewood, Colorado and London Reformed Baptist Seminary.

The title of his Ph.D. dissertation is *"The Anchor of a Believer's Hope: John Flavel's (ca. 1627–1691) Theology of Death, Dying, and Eternal Destiny,"* completed at Apeldoorn Theological Seminary, Netherlands, under the guidance of Dr. Herman Selderhuis.

Jason has served as preaching pastor since Christ Reformed Heritage Church in the Denver metro area, in 2021.